“D”etermination “R”elationships “U”nderstanding “M”entorship

Up Your Business...

The Keys To Success

by Bart Robley

ISBN 978-1-57424-426-7

P. O. Box 17878 - Anaheim Hills, CA 92817
email: centerstrm@aol.com • web: centerstream-usa.com

Dedication

To the memory of **Dom Famularo**, a true ambassador of drumming whose passion, wisdom, and boundless energy forever changed the face of our instrument. Dom's unwavering belief in the power of music made it possible for drummers around the world to chase their dreams, myself included.

I am deeply honored that he wrote the foreword to my book *The Rhythmic Journey*, and I carry his lessons, encouragement, and infectious spirit with me always.

In Dom's words, **"Onward and Upward!"**

Table of Contents

Chapter 1:
Determination - The Foundation of Success

When I first started out as a musician, I often heard people say, "You must be so inspired to do what you do." I smiled and nodded politely, but deep down, I knew that inspiration and motivation might get you started, but they won't keep you going when the road gets tough, and trust me, the road always gets tough. What kept me behind the drum kit, perfecting my craft, hustling for gigs, and showing up every single day wasn't inspiration or motivation. It was **determination**.

What Determination Really Means

Determination isn't glamorous. It doesn't look like the sparkly "aha!" moments you see in motivational speeches or Instagram posts. Determination is gritty. It's the decision to keep moving forward even when the path is unclear, the obstacles seem insurmountable, and every part of you wants to give up.

Here's the truth: inspiration and motivation are fleeting. They're great when they're there, but they can vanish as quickly as they appear. Determination, on the other hand, is a steady companion. It's the quiet resolve that whispers, "Keep going," when all you want to do is quit.

When you see a musician or a band performing at the top of their game, delivering a flawless performance that captivates the audience, you're witnessing the culmination of years of relentless effort, dedication, and sacrifice. What you see under the stage lights, the precision, passion, and artistry, is just the tip of the iceberg. Behind that moment of magic lies countless hours of practice, late nights, early mornings, and an unwavering commitment to their craft. It's easy to be swept up in the glitz and glamour of a great show, but the reality of how it comes together is anything but glamorous.

Most of a musician's journey happens far away from the stage, in rehearsal spaces, studios, and basements. It's filled with repetition, playing the same riff, drum fill, or vocal run over and over until it's ingrained in muscle memory. It's learning to play through mistakes, fatigue, and

Rich Redmond

frustration. There's nothing flashy about running scales for hours or practicing transitions until they're seamless, but this is where the magic is built. The process is gritty and, at times, exhausting, requiring discipline and determination to push through even when it feels like progress is slow or nonexistent.

Recently I spent some time with Rich Redmond at a party hosted by Sabian Cymbals at PASIC (Percussive Arts Society International Convention) in Indianapolis. Redmond has been the touring and recording drummer with multi-platinum country rocker Jason Aldean for nearly two decades. He has recorded 31#1 radio hits and plays to millions of fans per year in iconic venues across the globe. Rich has also worked with artists such as Kelly Clarkson, Carrie Underwood, Ludacris, Bryan Adams, Bob Seger, Chris Cornell, Miranda Lambert, Eric Church, Keith Urban, Luke Bryan and many more. Rich is also a busy educator, speaker, author, and actor. Check out his website at **www.richredmond.com**

When I told Rich I was writing a book titled "Drum Up Your Business" and that the opening chapter focused on determination, he simply said, " When motivation ends, determination picks up the slack." That was so simple, so perfect! I loved it!

Then there's the unspoken work that doesn't involve the music itself, loading gear in and out of venues, driving for hours (sometimes days) between gigs, managing schedules, and navigating the business side of things. Every successful musician has faced setbacks, from broken strings and technical failures to canceled gigs and financial struggles. They've had to learn how to adapt, problem-solve, and keep going when things didn't go as planned. These moments aren't what audiences think of when they imagine the life of a musician, but they're an integral part of what makes a band or artist great.

The truth is, the road to mastery isn't glamorous, it's down and dirty, full of sweat, sacrifice, and moments of doubt. But it's also incredibly rewarding. The hard work and resilience it takes to reach the top of your game create a depth of character and a profound appreciation for those fleeting moments when everything clicks. When you watch a band deliver an incredible performance, know that it's not just talent you're witnessing, it's a testament to their commitment, passion, and the grit it took to get there.

Successful entrepreneurs, like successful musicians, know this: when inspiration and motivation fail, and they will, it's determination that sees them through.

Setting Goals and Staying Focused

Determination without direction is like playing a drum solo without a tempo, it's chaotic and ultimately ineffective. That's where goal-setting comes in. Goals give your determination a purpose.

Start with clear, actionable goals. Instead of saying, "I want to grow my business," define exactly what that means: "I want to increase revenue by 25% this year by expanding into two new markets." Once you have a specific goal, break it into smaller, manageable steps.

Here's the secret to staying focused: keep your goals visible. Write them down, hang them on your wall, or set reminders on your phone. When you lose sight of your goals, it's easy to lose your resolve.

Remember, focus is a muscle, and like any muscle, it gets stronger with practice. Eliminate distractions, set aside dedicated time for deep work, and don't be afraid to say no to things that don't align with your goals.

In the music business, "work" isn't confined to rehearsals or performances, it's a multifaceted endeavor that encompasses everything from honing your craft to managing the administrative side of your career. Think of your practice time as a crucial part of your workday. Just like an athlete trains to stay in peak condition, musicians need regular, focused practice to maintain and improve their skills. Dedicate time each day to refining your technique, learning new material, or experimenting creatively. Treat this as non-negotiable "work time," because the progress you make behind the scenes directly impacts your success on stage or in the studio.

But work in the music industry doesn't stop at your instrument. Administrative tasks, like bookkeeping, are just as important. Tracking expenses, managing invoices, and staying on top of your finances may not feel glamorous, but it's essential for keeping your career running smoothly. Dedicate a portion of your week to organizing receipts, updating spreadsheets, or using financial tools to track your income and expenses. Staying on top of this ensures you're not scrambling during tax season and gives you a clear picture of your financial health, empowering you to make better decisions for your career.

Another vital component of your work is building and maintaining relationships, which often starts with outreach. Writing emails to potential endorsements, venues, or collaborators is an investment in your future. Crafting thoughtful, professional communication takes time, but it's worth the effort. Research the brands or individuals you're contacting, personalize your message, and clearly outline how a partnership would be mutually beneficial. Consistent, professional outreach is how you grow your network and create opportunities for endorsements, gigs, and collaborations. Remember, every email sent, every connection made, and every task completed outside of playing is a brick in the foundation of your career.

> **Define Clear Objectives:** *Establish specific, measurable, and achievable goals for your music career, such as completing an album, booking a certain number of gigs, or growing your online presence. Clear objectives provide a roadmap and keep your determination aligned with your vision.*

Defining clear objectives is a foundational step in building a successful music career, as it transforms your aspirations into actionable goals. Specific, measurable, and achievable objectives give you a tangible roadmap to follow, ensuring that your efforts are focused and purposeful. For example, rather than setting a vague goal like "become more successful," you could aim to complete an album within six months, secure at least two gigs per month, or grow your online audience by a specific percentage over the next quarter. These clearly defined targets make it easier to track

L to R: **Geln Sobel** (Alice Cooper), **Adam Parsons, Bart and Joey Scott** (Lizzy Bordan)

your progress and maintain motivation as you achieve each milestone. They also help you prioritize tasks and allocate your time effectively, ensuring that every action you take aligns with your long-term vision. Clear objectives not only fuel your determination but also allow you to measure success and adapt your strategy as needed, keeping you firmly on the path toward achieving your dreams.

> **Break Goals into Actionable Steps:** *Divide larger goals into smaller, manageable tasks, such as writing one song a week or dedicating specific hours to practice or networking. This approach helps you stay focused and maintain consistent progress without feeling overwhelmed.*

Breaking goals into actionable steps is a powerful way to make progress without feeling overwhelmed, and it can be likened to the saying, "How do you eat an elephant? One bite at a time." Large, intimidating goals, like recording an album or launching a tour, can seem unachievable at first glance. However, when you break them down into smaller, more manageable tasks, they become less daunting. For instance, instead of focusing on the enormity of creating an entire album, you might set a goal to write one song per week or dedicate specific hours each day to practice or networking. These smaller steps not only make the goal feel more achievable, but they also help you maintain momentum and stay focused on consistent progress. By taking things one step at a time, you're able to build a sense of accomplishment and stay on track toward your larger objectives, without getting lost in the big picture.

Prioritize and Eliminate Distractions: *Identify the most important tasks that contribute directly to your goals and allocate time to them. Avoid activities or habits that detract from your focus, such as excessive social media use or over-committing to non-essential projects.*

Prioritizing and eliminating distractions is key to maintaining focus and making consistent progress toward your music career goals. Start by identifying the tasks that will have the greatest impact on your success, whether it's writing new music, preparing for a big performance, or networking with industry professionals. Once you've pinpointed these high-priority tasks, allocate dedicated time for them in your schedule, ensuring that you are actively working toward your objectives. At the same time, it's important to recognize and avoid activities that divert your attention away from your priorities, such as spending excessive time on social media, engaging in unnecessary meetings, or over-committing to projects that don't directly support your goals. By setting boundaries and cutting out time-wasting habits, you can fully invest your energy in the tasks that matter most. This intentional approach to time management allows you to stay focused, minimize stress, and maximize your productivity, ultimately leading you to greater success in your music career.

Monitor Progress and Adjust Plans: *Regularly evaluate your progress and celebrate milestones to stay motivated. If obstacles arise, adapt your plans without losing sight of your overall objectives, maintaining the determination to keep moving forward.*

Monitoring your progress and adjusting your plans along the way is essential for staying on track and ensuring continued growth in your music career. Regularly assessing how far you've come allows you to celebrate milestones, whether it's finishing a song, landing a new gig, or increasing your social media following. These moments of recognition serve as powerful motivators, helping you stay inspired and committed to your long-term goals. However, it's also important to remain flexible when obstacles arise. Unexpected challenges, such as scheduling conflicts or creative blocks, can derail your plans temporarily. Instead of letting these setbacks throw you off course, view them as opportunities to adjust your approach. For example, if a recording deadline is missed, break down the project into smaller tasks to ensure you stay focused on completion. By maintaining a solution-oriented mindset and adapting your strategy as needed, you keep your determination intact and stay aligned with your overall objectives, ensuring that you continue to move forward, even in the face of adversity.

Overcoming Challenges and Persevering Through Adversity

Let's face it, failure is inevitable. You will encounter setbacks, disappointments, and moments where nothing seems to go your way. It's how you respond to those moments that define your success.

When I broke into the music industry, rejection was constant. For every gig I landed, there were ten I didn't. But I learned to see challenges as opportunities to grow. Instead of asking, "Why me?" I started asking, "What can I learn from this?"

In the music business or any industry, hearing "no" is inevitable. It can feel personal, discouraging, and even like a sign to give up. But the truth is, "no" is rarely the end of the road; it's just a redirection. The key to overcoming rejection is shifting your perspective. Instead of seeing "no" as a failure, view it as an opportunity to learn, adapt, and refine your approach. Maybe your pitch needs tweaking, your timing was off, or the person you reached out to simply wasn't the right fit. Rejections are stepping stones that build resilience and teach valuable lessons about perseverance. Every "no" you hear gets you closer to the right "yes," as long as you stay determined, stay professional, and keep moving forward. Use rejection as fuel to keep improving because the most successful people in the world have all been told "no" countless times, and they didn't let it stop them.

The music business is a journey filled with incredible highs, but also plenty of rejection. Every "no" you hear, whether from a record label, a potential collaborator, a venue, or getting turned down by a company you want to endorse it's not the end of the road. These are stepping stones to success. It took me three attempts to finally get my endorsement with Gretsch drums.

These moments test your dedication and resilience, reminding you that even the greatest artists faced their share of setbacks before breaking through. Rejection often teaches us more than success, offering a chance to reflect, adapt, and grow stronger. It's a natural part of the creative process, pushing you to refine your craft, build thicker skin, and develop the determination needed to thrive in such a competitive industry.

Hearing "no" should fuel your resolve, not diminish it. Use it as a motivator to work harder, prove doubters wrong, and elevate your game. Remember, every rejection brings you one step closer to the right opportunity, and every closed door prepares you to appreciate the open ones even more. Resilience is the cornerstone of success in the music business, and the ability to persist in the face of rejection sets apart those who merely dream from those who achieve. Stay true to your vision, trust your talent, and let every setback be the foundation upon which you build an unstoppable career.

Challenges are not roadblocks; they're stepping stones. Each obstacle you overcome builds your resilience and sharpens your skills. Embrace adversity, because it's where the real growth happens.

Building a Resilient Mindset

At the heart of determination lies resilience, the ability to bounce back from setbacks and keep moving forward. Resilience isn't something you're born with; it's something you build.

Start by cultivating a growth mindset. Believe that your abilities and intelligence can be developed through hard work, learning, and persistence. Avoid the trap of thinking, "I'm just not good at this." Instead, tell yourself, "I'm not good at this yet."

Resilience is the backbone of success in any pursuit, especially in the unpredictable world of the music business. It's the ability to bounce back from setbacks, adapt to challenges, and keep moving forward when the odds seem stacked against you. Resilience doesn't mean ignoring pain or disappointment; it means acknowledging them and choosing to persevere despite them. Whether it's facing rejection, losing an opportunity, or navigating a tough financial period, resilience is what allows you to weather the storm and come out stronger on the other side. Without it, even the most talented and hardworking individuals can falter when confronted with adversity.

The importance of resilience lies not only in surviving challenges but also in thriving because of them. Each obstacle you overcome adds to your skill set, sharpens your problem-solving abilities, and builds your confidence. Resilient people understand that failure is not the opposite of success, it's part of the process. By embracing setbacks as opportunities to learn and grow, you transform hardships into stepping stones toward your goals. Resilience also sets an example for others, inspiring your team, collaborators, or audience to adopt a similar mindset. In a world where the ability to adapt is more critical than ever, resilience is the key to staying relevant, focused, and unshakeable.

Practice self-compassion. You're going to make mistakes, and that's okay. Don't let failure define you. Use it as fuel to keep going.

For the longest time, I didn't understand what self-compassion was, let alone why it mattered. I thought being hard on myself, relentlessly critiquing my performances, pushing through exhaustion, and never allowing room for mistakes, was the only way to grow. But over time, I realized that this mindset wasn't driving me forward; it was holding me back. When I made a mistake, I'd beat myself up instead of learning from it. When things didn't go as planned, I'd blame myself instead of recognizing external factors or simply acknowledging that setbacks are part of the process. It wasn't until I embraced self-compassion that I began to truly grow, not just as a musician or entrepreneur, but as a person.

Practicing self-compassion means treating yourself with the same kindness and understanding that you'd offer a close friend. It's about recognizing that perfection isn't possible, and that's okay. When you show yourself compassion, you create space to learn from your mistakes rather than being paralyzed by them. It also helps you stay resilient when the going gets tough because instead of adding to the weight of challenges with self-criticism, you lighten the load with encouragement and perspective. Self-compassion doesn't make you weak or complacent, it gives you the strength to keep going, the patience to improve, and the confidence to face whatever comes next. It's a lesson I wish I'd learned sooner, but one I'm grateful to carry forward now.

People Who Lift You Up

Surround yourself with people who lift you up. Whether it's a mentor, a supportive community, or a trusted friend, having someone in your corner makes all the difference.

Surrounding yourself with people who lift you up is one of the most powerful choices you can make for your personal and professional growth. These individuals provide encouragement, perspective, and strength when you need it most, serving as a reminder that you're never alone in your journey. Whether it's a mentor offering guidance, a supportive community sharing wisdom, or a trusted friend cheering you on, having the right people in your corner can turn even the most daunting challenges into manageable stepping stones. They help you see possibilities where you might only see roadblocks and celebrate your victories, big and small as if they were their own.

For me, my wife has been there through so much. She has stood by me when most people would have kicked me to the curb. I've also found support in my bandmates and the members of The Drummers Education Connection (DEC). My bandmates are like family, our shared passion for music fuels my drive and reminds me of the joy in what we do together. The "DEC" community has become an incredible source of inspiration and collaboration, full of people who understand the ups and downs of our shared industry and genuinely want to see each other succeed. These relationships have not only enriched my career but also brought incredible depth to my life.

Having people who believe in you creates a ripple effect of positivity and productivity. Their energy and support make it easier to persevere through tough times and motivate you to strive for excellence. Surrounding yourself with people who lift you up doesn't just impact your work; it shapes your mindset and encourages you to become the best version of yourself. By fostering these connections, you also create a foundation of trust and collaboration that enriches both your career and your life. Remember, the people you choose to surround yourself with can either drain you or elevate you; choose wisely.

> **Positive Energy and Motivation:** *Being around uplifting individuals fosters a positive environment that boosts your morale, keeping you motivated to tackle challenges and stay determined.*

Positive energy is contagious, and being surrounded by uplifting individuals creates an environment where you feel encouraged and inspired. These people radiate optimism and remind you to focus on opportunities instead of obstacles. Their positive outlook can shift your mindset, making challenges feel more manageable and achievable. When you're motivated by others' encouragement and enthusiasm, it becomes easier to maintain your determination and work towards your goals with confidence. The energy you absorb from positive influences can be the difference between feeling stuck and finding the drive to keep moving forward.

Moreover, uplifting individuals help foster a sense of belonging and support that strengthens your resilience. Their belief in your abilities serves as a powerful motivator, pushing you to persevere even in the face of adversity. This positive environment can also spark creativity and new ideas, as you feel inspired to take on challenges with a fresh perspective. The encouragement and constructive feedback they provide help you stay focused and committed, ensuring that you remain determined and energized to achieve your aspirations.

> **Encouragement During Setbacks:** *Supportive people provide encouragement when you encounter obstacles, helping you maintain focus and avoid giving up on your goals.*

Setbacks are inevitable on the path to achieving your goals, but having supportive people around you can make all the difference in how you handle them. These individuals offer encouragement during tough times, reminding you of your strengths and past successes. Their belief in your ability to overcome challenges helps you stay focused on the bigger picture, rather than getting lost in temporary setbacks. Knowing that someone has your back can be a powerful motivator, giving you the resilience to push through obstacles and continue striving toward your aspirations.

Supportive people also provide valuable perspective during difficult times, helping you see setbacks as learning opportunities rather than failures. They can offer advice, share their own experiences, or simply lend a listening ear, all of which can alleviate feelings of frustration or self-doubt. This encouragement not only prevents you from giving up but also reinforces your determination to keep moving forward. With their support, you're more likely to view obstacles as part of the journey and maintain the confidence needed to achieve your goals

> **Inspiration Through Example:** *Surrounding yourself with driven and positive people inspires you to emulate their habits, mindset, and resilience, reinforcing your own determination.*

Being around driven and positive individuals provides a constant source of inspiration through their actions and attitudes. Observing their habits, such as discipline, time management, and perseverance, can motivate you to adopt similar practices in your own life. Their resilience in overcoming challenges demonstrates that success is achievable with effort and persistence. By witnessing their dedication and progress, you naturally feel encouraged to follow in their footsteps, reinforcing your own determination to reach your goals.

Additionally, these individuals often possess a growth-oriented mindset, viewing setbacks as opportunities to learn and improve. Their ability to stay optimistic and focused in the face of adversity is contagious, fostering a similar mindset in you. This shared energy creates a cycle of inspiration where you continuously uplift and motivate one another. By emulating their behaviors and attitudes, you not only enhance your personal growth but also build a strong foundation for long-term success and determination.

> **Accountability and Growth:** *Encouraging friends or colleagues to hold you accountable to your commitments, helping you stay on track and pushing you to achieve your best.*

For professional musicians, accountability is a cornerstone of growth and success. Surrounding yourself with supportive colleagues or friends who hold you accountable ensures you stay committed to your practice routines, deadlines, and creative goals. Whether it's preparing for a performance, meeting recording commitments, or maintaining a consistent presence in your music career, having others to check in with motivates you to follow through. Their constructive feedback helps identify areas for improvement, pushing you to refine your craft and reach your full potential. Accountability not only keeps you on track but also fosters a sense of discipline that is essential in the competitive world of music.

Growth in music is a continuous journey, and the encouragement of peers is invaluable in helping you stay inspired and resilient. Collaborating with other musicians or mentors who challenge you to explore new techniques, genres, or ideas helps you expand your skill set and artistic vision. These relationships provide a safe space to experiment, learn, and grow, while also ensuring you maintain high standards in your work. By embracing accountability and seeking out growth opportunities with others, you can achieve greater consistency and creativity, ultimately enhancing your career as a professional musician.

> **Confidence and Self-Belief:** *Supportive relationships build your confidence and self-belief by reminding you of your strengths and celebrating your progress, fueling your determination to succeed.*

In the music business, confidence and self-belief are essential qualities that fuel success and supportive relationships play a crucial role in nurturing these traits. The competitive nature of the industry can often lead to self-doubt, but having people who remind you of your strengths and accomplishments can counteract that negativity. Whether it's a bandmate complimenting your performance or a mentor praising your dedication, these affirmations reinforce your belief in your abilities. This boost in confidence helps you approach your craft and career decisions with greater assurance, allowing you to seize opportunities and take creative risks.

Supportive relationships also provide a network of encouragement during moments of uncertainty or rejection, which are inevitable in the music industry. Whether it's a missed audition, a less-than-perfect performance, or critical feedback, these individuals help you see setbacks as stepping stones rather than failures. By celebrating your progress and milestones, no matter how small, they keep you focused on the bigger picture and remind you of how far you've come. This steady encouragement strengthens your determination, ensuring you stay committed to your goals even when the path is challenging.

Furthermore, confidence and self-belief are contagious in a creative environment. When you feel supported, it reflects in your performances, compositions, and collaborations. This energy can inspire others in your circle, creating a cycle of positivity and mutual motivation. With a strong foundation of self-belief, you're more likely to pursue ambitious projects, connect authentically with your audience, and build lasting relationships in the music business. Ultimately, these supportive connections become a vital resource for sustaining your passion and determination in a demanding industry.

It's All About the Follow-Through

In the music business, finishing a project requires more than just completing the big tasks; it's about the follow-through, the attention

L to R: **Bart, Chris Brady** (Aquarian Artist Relations), **Dusty Watson** (Nashville Pussy Dick Dale, The Sonics, Lita Ford)

to the small details that ensure the project is truly done. Whether it's a gig, a recording session, writing an album, or building a studio, the final stages often require extra effort and determination. It's easy to feel satisfied when the major parts of a project are finished, but that's often when the real work begins. Small elements like final edits, adjustments to mixes, or rehearsals before a show may seem insignificant at first, but they can make the difference between a good project and a great one. The key to success in the music industry is being willing to push through those final steps, even when it feels like the finish line is already in sight.

When recording an album, for example, it's tempting to think the work is done once the tracks are laid down. However, the devil is in the details, mixing, mastering, and sequencing all require time and precision to ensure the best possible sound. Without this final touch, an album can feel incomplete, even if the songs are great. It's easy to overlook these finishing tasks, especially if you're eager to move on to the next project, but determination during these stages ensures the end product lives up to its full potential. Just as a song isn't truly finished until it's fully mixed and mastered, a project in any form of music requires a commitment to follow-through, seeing each detail through to completion.

Similarly, with live performances, follow-through means not just showing up on time but ensuring the sound is right, the setlist is rehearsed, and the crowd is engaged. It can be tempting to take shortcuts, especially after a long day of rehearsals or travel, but making sure every aspect of the performance is polished shows your professionalism and dedication to the craft. The same determination that got you to the stage in the first place needs to carry through until the last note is played. The final impression you leave on the audience is often shaped by the last-minute details that show you care about giving them your best.

Writing a book or creating educational content in the music business, like a drum method book or instructional DVD, also relies heavily on follow-through. The process may start with enthusiasm, but the challenge lies in maintaining that energy to the end. Drafting content, revising, formatting, and preparing for publication all require commitment. Many times, the initial excitement wanes as the project drags on, and the temptation to cut corners or rush through the final stages can undermine the effort. However, the determination to follow through and make sure the final product is polished, accurate, and professional is what separates successful musicians and educators from those who don't finish what they started.

Building a studio or any large-scale project in the music business also demands an unyielding commitment to the details. While it's easy to imagine the final result, a fully functioning, top-of-the-line recording space, there are countless small decisions to be made. Whether it's choosing the right gear, optimizing the acoustics, or ensuring the environment is comfortable and inspiring, it takes determination to bring the vision to life. The follow-through is where the project really takes shape, and the effort you put into these finishing touches is what will make your studio a place where you can produce your best work, time and time again. In every area of the music business, following through with attention to detail is what transforms a good project into an exceptional one.

The Steady Beat of Determination

Determination is the steady beat that keeps the music of your business alive. It's not flashy or exciting, but it's essential. Without it, the rhythm falters, and the melody falls apart.

As you embark on your entrepreneurial journey, remember this: you don't need to feel inspired every day. You don't need to be motivated every moment. What you do need is the resolve to keep moving forward, one step at a time, even when it's hard, especially when it's hard.

Determination is the foundation of success. Build it, nurture it, and let it carry you through the highs and lows. The rest of this book will give you the tools to complement your determination, but this is where it all begins. So, take a deep breath, set your tempo, and let determination lead the way.

It's easy to get caught up in the excitement of new ideas, products, or opportunities, but it's the consistency of determination that keeps you on track. It's not the flashy bursts of inspiration that propel you forward but the quiet, steadfast commitment to your goals, even when external circumstances shift. Like the steady beat of a metronome, determination ensures that you maintain your course and rhythm, no matter how chaotic the world around you may become.

In the early days of entrepreneurship, motivation can be fleeting, and inspiration may feel like a distant memory. But that's okay. You don't have to feel energized or creative every moment of every day. What matters is the perseverance to keep going when the road gets tough, the resilience to press on when the odds are against you, and the discipline to keep working toward your goals despite setbacks. The beauty of determination is that it doesn't rely on the highs of emotion or fleeting bursts of energy; it's a quiet, dependable force that compels you to keep pushing, no matter the obstacles.

At the core of every successful business is determination. It's the bedrock that will help you weather the storms and celebrate the victories. Along the way, you'll encounter moments that test your resolve, but these are the very moments that will shape you as an entrepreneur. In the chapters ahead, you'll gain valuable tools and insights to build on your determination and enhance your business. But remember, all the strategies and techniques in the world won't matter unless you have the grit to keep moving forward. So, set your pace, stay focused, and let determination be your guide as you navigate the journey ahead.

Chapter 2:
Relationships: The Heart of Your Business

In the music business, technical skills and talent open the door, but relationships keep you in the room. Your ability to connect, collaborate, and build trust with others forms the bedrock of a sustainable and successful career. This chapter explores how to network with purpose, cultivate meaningful connections, and create lasting partnerships that drive your business forward.

Networking with Purpose

Networking is more than just collecting business cards or adding contacts to your phone. It's about intentionality, seeking out connections that align with your goals and values. Before attending events, ask yourself:

What do I hope to achieve? *Whether it's finding a mentor, securing a gig, or learning about a new opportunity, clarity will guide your interactions. When you know what you want, you can approach conversations with focus and confidence. For instance, if your goal is to find a mentor, you might prepare questions about their journey and seek advice on how to navigate challenges in your career. If you're looking for a gig, you can highlight your skills and experience tailored to the opportunities at hand. Clear objectives not only help you articulate your needs but also make it easier for others to see how they can support you. Understanding your goals ensures that every interaction has a purpose, making the time spent networking both productive and meaningful.*

Who can I help? *Approach networking with a mindset of giving, not just taking. Offering value builds goodwill and opens doors for future collaboration. My podcast, The Drummers Education Connection, is a prime example of this principle in action. Through networking and mentoring, the podcast provides a platform to help other drummers connect, learn, and grow in their craft. By sharing knowledge and experiences, we create a supportive community that fosters growth and opportunity for everyone involved.*

Practical steps for purposeful networking:

> **Research before you reach out.** *Learn about the people you want to connect with, their work, and how you can add value to their lives.*
>
> **Prepare your elevator pitch.** *Be ready to succinctly share who you are, what you do, and what you're looking for. No one wants to hear someone "sell" them during a pitch. They want to feel connected, not sold. Focus on fostering a sense of shared interests and authenticity, which builds rapport and trust far more effectively than a rehearsed sales pitch.*
>
> **Follow up.** *Via text, email, or call, ensure your follow-up is timely and considerate. Show gratitude for the interaction and reference specific details from your conversation. Approach follow-ups in a friendly, non-pushy manner, and be respectful of their time and space. Space out your communication and watch for cues to gauge their interest in continuing the dialogue. Remember, the goal is to stay on their radar without becoming a source of irritation.*

Building relationships is the cornerstone of success in the music industry. While your talent and skill on the drums are essential, they're often just the baseline for getting noticed. Networking, connecting meaningfully with other musicians, producers, and industry professionals, is where real opportunities arise. Collaborations, gigs, and referrals often come not from cold calls or emails but from relationships built on trust and mutual respect. The phrase "NETWORK NETWORK NETWORK!" cannot be overstated, your ability to foster genuine connections is as critical as your ability to keep time behind the kit.

Effective networking, however, isn't just about what you can gain. The most successful relationships are reciprocal, built on how you can help others as much as they can help you. By offering value, whether it's lending a hand on a project, sharing a contact, or even just showing up to support a friend's performance, you create a positive reputation that encourages others to think of you when opportunities arise. Adopt the mindset that it's better to give than to receive; in doing so, you'll not only build a stronger network but also a community of like-minded professionals who want to see you succeed.

Cultivating Meaningful Connections

Building relationships in the music business isn't a one-and-done task. It requires consistent effort and authenticity. Here's how to cultivate connections that last:

Show genuine interest. Ask thoughtful questions about others' projects, goals, and challenges. Active listening demonstrates respect and care. Again, business is about relationships, building the relationship and a possible friendship. By fostering a personal connection, you lay the foundation for trust and mutual support, which can lead to both professional and personal growth.

Be present. Ask thoughtful questions about others' projects, goals, and challenges. Active listening demonstrates respect and care. Again, business is about relationships, building relationship, and a possible friendship. Stay away from being distracted by phone calls, texts, or social media during conversations. Giving someone your full attention shows that you value their time and fosters a deeper connection. By fostering a personal connection, you lay the foundation for trust and mutual support, which can lead to both professional and personal growth.

Stay in touch. Check in periodically to see how someone is doing, share helpful resources celebrate their wins. Consistent communication keeps relationships warm and meaningful. A text, phone call, or email can go a long way in showing you care. Sometimes a simple "Hello, how are you?" or a thoughtful holiday greeting is all it takes to strengthen not only the business relationship but also build a lasting friendship. Personal touches like remembering important dates, milestones, or shared interests can make your connections feel valued and appreciated. Ultimately, maintaining relationships with genuine care and regular outreach fosters trust, loyalty, and mutual respect.

Building Trust with Clients and Colleagues

Trust is the currency of all successful relationships. Without it, even the most talented musician or businessperson will struggle to thrive. To build trust:

Deliver on your promises. *Reliability is key. If you commit to a deadline, a project, or an engagement, make it your priority to follow through.*

Whether you're performing a gig, attending a rehearsal, or participating in a recording session, always be on time and well-prepared. Know the material, bring the correct instrument for the job, and be mentally and physically ready to give your best performance. If you're giving lessons, show the same level of professionalism. Be punctual, and don't make the student wait, their time is just as valuable as yours. Consistently delivering on your promises builds trust and shows you value both your commitments and the people you're working with. This level of professionalism will not only enhance your reputation but also solidify your relationships with clients, students, and peers.

Be transparent. *Honesty about your capabilities, limitations, and expectations fosters respect. If you're called to perform in a genre you're not familiar with, say, a Latin jazz gig, and you've never attempted to play a Bossa Nova, it's crucial to be upfront about it. Taking on something outside your expertise without proper preparation will not only make you look like a fool but also reflect poorly on the person who hired you and trusted you to deliver. Transparency ensures that both you and the client can set realistic expectations and avoid disappointments. It's better to pass on an opportunity or ask for additional preparation time than to risk compromising your reputation and the quality of the performance. Building trust through honest communication strengthens relationships and positions you as a reliable and professional artist.*

Communicate effectively. *Keep lines of communication open and professional. Whether it's a quick update or addressing a challenge, clarity and consistency build confidence. Effective communication is the backbone of any successful business relationship, whether with clients, employees, partners, or suppliers. Clear, concise, and consistent communication fosters trust and ensures that everyone involved is on the same page. When you make it a habit to communicate openly, you not only prevent misunderstandings but also create a sense of transparency that builds confidence in your professionalism. When challenges arise, how you address them speaks volumes about your leadership and approach to problem-solving. Keeping lines of communication open ensures that issues are addressed promptly and efficiently before they escalate into bigger problems. Being proactive in your communication, rather than waiting for someone to bring up concerns, shows that you're engaged and invested in the success of the business. This* *proactive approach can significantly enhance your credibility and establish you as a dependable leader.*

The Power of Collaboration

No one achieves success in isolation. Collaboration allows you to tap into diverse skills, perspectives, and networks. Here's how to make the most of collaborative opportunities:

Find the right partners. *Look for collaborators who complement your strengths and share your vision.*

Finding the right partners is a cornerstone of success in the music industry, whether you're forming a band, writing songs, or launching a broader musical endeavor. Partners who complement your strengths bring skills and perspectives that fill gaps in your abilities, creating a well-rounded team. For instance, a songwriter with a gift for crafting melodies might partner with a lyricist whose words bring those melodies to life. By sharing a common vision, you ensure that your collaboration moves in a cohesive direction, minimizing potential conflicts and maximizing creative synergy. The key is to seek out individuals who not only bring technical expertise but also share your passion and long-term goals.

When starting a band, this principle becomes even more critical as the collaboration extends beyond the music itself. Bandmates often need to navigate the business side of the industry together, handling tasks like promotion, booking gigs, and managing finances. Each member's unique skills can be instrumental in these areas, a bassist with a knack for graphic design might create the band's visuals, while a drummer with social media savvy could manage the online presence. Working with partners who align with your vision ensures that these efforts reflect your shared identity, fostering a sense of unity both on and off the stage.

Moreover, collaboration at this deeper level requires trust, communication, and mutual respect. The music business is often unpredictable and challenging, and having partners who are equally committed to weathering the ups and downs is invaluable. A strong team can navigate creative differences and business hurdles with resilience, turning challenges into opportunities. By finding collaborators who not only complement your strengths but also share your work ethic and values, you're setting the foundation for a lasting and fruitful partnership that enhances both your music and your career trajectory.

> **Define roles and expectations.** *Clear agreements upfront prevent misunderstandings and ensure everyone is on the same page.*

Defining roles and expectations is a fundamental step in any music collaboration, whether it's forming a band or teaming up for songwriting. Clear agreements made upfront set the tone for the partnership, establishing who is responsible for what and how decisions will be made. For instance, in a band, you might designate one member to handle booking gigs, another to manage social media, and someone else to oversee finances. Similarly, in a songwriting collaboration, you might agree on how royalties will be split or who has the final say on edits. These agreements prevent confusion and misunderstandings, allowing the group to focus on creating and performing rather than navigating conflicts.

Beyond task allocation, defining expectations also helps ensure that everyone shares a common vision for the project. This includes clarifying creative goals, commitment levels, and timelines. For example, does everyone agree on the type of music you'll create, the frequency of rehearsals, or the intensity of touring schedules? Putting these details in writing, whether in a formal contract or a simple agreement, provides a reference point for the group to revisit if disputes arise. Ultimately, clear communication and defined roles foster a professional and productive working environment, ensuring that all members feel valued and that the project runs smoothly.

> **Celebrate shared successes.** *Recognize and appreciate each contributor's efforts. This not only strengthens relationships but also encourages future collaborations.*

Celebrating shared successes is an essential practice in any music collaboration. Whether it's the completion of a new song, a successful gig, or hitting a milestone like releasing an album, taking the time to recognize the collective achievement strengthens the bonds between collaborators. Acknowledging the unique contributions of each member highlights the value they bring to the team, reinforcing mutual respect and camaraderie. For example, praising a bassist for their groove or a lyricist for their poignant lines ensures that everyone feels seen and appreciated. These moments

L to R: **Nick D'Virgilio, Ted Morton, and Bart**

of celebration create positive memories that can carry the group through tougher times.

By openly recognizing and appreciating each contributor's efforts, you foster a culture of gratitude and respect. This approach helps to ensure that no one feels overshadowed or undervalued. Celebrations can take many forms, from a simple toast after a successful show to a more formal acknowledgment in liner notes or public statements. Such gestures prevent resentment from building, as they make it clear that everyone's role is important. When people feel valued, they are more likely to stay engaged and motivated, ensuring the project continues to thrive and that future collaborations remain appealing.

Moreover, celebrating successes together lays the foundation for a healthy, sustainable working relationship. It creates a sense of shared ownership and pride in the accomplishments of the group. This not only boosts morale but also sets the stage for smoother teamwork in future projects. When collaborators know their efforts will be recognized, they're more likely to invest their energy and creativity fully, leading to even greater achievements. Ultimately, taking the time to celebrate doesn't just acknowledge the present moment; it builds trust and enthusiasm for what lies ahead, making sure no one feels their contributions are overlooked or their toes stepped on.

Endorsement Deals: A Partnership Built on Relationships

The foundation of any successful endorsement deal is trust and communication. Here are some tips to build and maintain these vital relationships.

When many musicians hear the term "endorsement deal," they imagine receiving free gear from a company in exchange for slapping their logo on stage or in photos. But the reality is far more nuanced and far more meaningful. At its core, an endorsement deal is not about freebies; it's about building a relationship rooted in mutual respect, shared values, and a common vision for success.

Endorsement deals are partnerships. When a company chooses to endorse an artist, they're not just giving away products; they're investing in someone who can authentically represent their brand. Likewise, when an artist enters into an endorsement deal, they're aligning themselves with a company whose products they genuinely believe in and are proud to use.

The Artist's Role

As an artist, your role in an endorsement deal goes beyond being a "poster child" for the brand. It's your responsibility to demonstrate why the company's products are essential to your craft. Whether through social media posts, interviews, live performances, or educational content, you become a storyteller, sharing how the gear enhances your music and your journey as an artist.

For example, if you've ever watched a drummer showcase their favorite cymbals or discuss the intricacies of their custom drumsticks, you've witnessed the power of this partnership. Those conversations aren't scripted sales pitches, they're authentic testimonials from artists who use those products to create their art.

The Company's Role

On the flip side, the company's role is to support the artist in their endeavors. This support might come in the form of discounted gear, promotional opportunities, or collaboration on projects. But at the heart of it, the company is betting on the artist's ability to inspire others to explore their products. They're also seeking feedback from the artist to improve and innovate their offerings.

For instance, many signature products, from cymbals to drumsticks to microphones, are born out of close collaboration between artists and manufacturers. These products are a testament to the deep relationship between the two parties, merging the artist's expertise with the company's technical know-how.

Be Genuine

Don't pursue an endorsement deal with a company just because they're popular. Align yourself with brands whose products you genuinely love and use. Over the years, I've had friends ask me to "hook them up" with an endorsement deal. They'll say something like, "Hey man, I know you're in tight with company X. Can you get me a deal?" I'm all about helping my fellow drummers out, so I have no problem going to bat for someone. But I always ask, "What model of widget do you use from company X?" If I get an answer that makes it clear they have no idea about the brand, I won't even think of representing them to the company. However, if they know the brand and it's obvious they use and believe in the products, I'm much more likely to help them out. Endorsements should always come from a place of authenticity and genuine connection with the gear.

Deliver Value

Think about how you can contribute to the company's goals. Are you willing to create content, participate in clinics, or provide feedback on product development? Endorsement deals are partnerships where artists and companies align their goals for mutual benefit. To secure and maintain such relationships, it's crucial to deliver value beyond simply using the product. Consider how you can actively contribute to the company's objectives. Are you prepared to create engaging content showcasing their products, participate in clinics to educate and inspire others, or provide thoughtful feedback to enhance product development? By demonstrating your willingness to be an active collaborator and advocate for the brand, you strengthen the partnership and ensure it remains beneficial for both parties.

Communicate Regularly

Keep the lines of communication open. Share updates about your projects, tours, and any exposure you're giving the brand. Don't wait for the company to reach out to you. Effective communication is a cornerstone of successful endorsement deals in the music industry. Regularly update the company on your projects, tours, and any opportunities where their brand is gaining visibility through your work. Share milestones, promotional content, and behind-the-scenes insights that showcase their products in action. By proactively reaching out instead of waiting for them to initiate contact, you demonstrate professionalism, enthusiasm, and a genuine commitment to the partnership. Open communication not only builds trust but also ensures both parties are aligned in maximizing the value of the endorsement.

Express Gratitude

Always show appreciation for the support you receive. A simple thank-you can go a long way in strengthening your partnership. Gratitude is a powerful force, not just in endorsement deals or the music business, but in life itself. Expressing appreciation for the support you receive can deepen connections and strengthen relationships. A heartfelt "thank you" is more than just polite; it's a way of acknowledging the effort, belief, and investment others have made in you. As drummer and business coach Matt Starr wisely put it, "Gratitude is the grease." It keeps the wheels of collaboration and mutual respect turning smoothly. Whether you're thanking a sponsor, a bandmate, or a loved one, a little gratitude can open doors, foster goodwill, and create lasting bonds that enrich both your personal and professional life.

Don't Be a Dick: The Golden Rule of the Music Business

When I interviewed Mitch Marine, drummer for country legend Dwight Yoakam, I asked him, "What's the key to success in the music business?" Without hesitation, he replied, "Don't be a dick." It's simple, direct, and true. Talent will open doors, but your attitude determines whether they stay open. No matter how skilled you are as a musician, being unpleasant or difficult to work with can quickly overshadow your abilities. A great attitude, on the other hand, can make you the kind of person everyone wants to have on their team.

Ask any bandleader or musical director, and they'll likely confirm this truth: they'd rather hire someone who is reliable, gets the job done, and is enjoyable to be around than a virtuoso who is insufferable. Touring and performing aren't just about playing music; they're about relationships. On the road, you spend hours traveling, living, and working in close quarters with the same group of people. A bad attitude or abrasive personality can make an already demanding lifestyle unbearable for everyone involved.

Being easy to work with isn't just about avoiding conflict, it's about being a team player. Respect others' time and contributions, be adaptable to different situations, and approach every gig with humility and gratitude. Remember, your reputation travels faster than you do in this industry, and word gets around. If you're known as someone who is dependable, kind, and fun to work with, you'll find doors opening that might otherwise have stayed closed. Ultimately, being a good hang can be just as important as playing the perfect groove.

Commitment Through Thick and Thin

Being part of a band isn't just about showing up to play; it's about building a family. For 26 years, I've been the drummer for The Sam Morrison Band, and in that time, we've navigated every imaginable twist and turn of life together. From flat tires on the road to personal battles like divorces and addiction, we've weathered the storms and celebrated the triumphs. The old saying "The strong will survive" couldn't be more fitting for the bond we've built. This level of commitment doesn't happen by chance, it's the result of consistently showing up for each other, no matter the circumstances.

True bandmates are there for the successes and the failures, the easy gigs and the hard times. Whether it's cheering each other on after a great show or lending a hand when life takes an unexpected turn, the strength of a band lies in its unity. Being a fair-weather member, someone who only sticks around for the good times erodes that trust and camaraderie. If you want to build something that lasts, you need to be there, fully present, fully engaged, and ready to face the ups and downs together. That's how you create more than just a band; you create a legacy.

Level Each Other Up!

One of the most rewarding aspects of collaborating with my fellow members of The Drummers Education Connection podcast is how we constantly level each other up. In every conversation, whether on-air or behind the scenes, we're not just sharing knowledge, we're inspiring each other to reach greater heights. Each of us brings unique expertise and experiences to the table, and that diversity creates a fertile ground for growth. When one of us shares a new teaching method, a fresh approach to drumming, or an innovative way to engage with students, it sparks something in the rest of us. This mutual encouragement isn't just about professional improvement; it's about becoming better educators, musicians, and individuals.

The motivation doesn't stop at inspiration; we actively challenge each other to push beyond our comfort zones. Whether it's trying a new piece of gear, experimenting with a different teaching platform, or setting ambitious goals for our playing, we hold each other accountable to take those next steps. This dynamic creates an upward spiral of growth, where each member's success becomes fuel for the others. The connection we share reminds me that collaboration isn't just about working together; it's about elevating each other. Through the DEC podcast, we've built more than a team, we've cultivated a community that thrives on mutual support and shared progress.

Don't Be A Yeah Butter

In any collaborative environment, one of the biggest roadblocks to progress is the "Yeah Butter" mentality. You know the type, the person who, no matter what idea or suggestion is presented, is ready to respond with "Yeah, but..." or "No, but..." or just outright negativity. This kind of attitude does nothing to move a group forward. Instead, it drains energy and stifles creativity. As someone who has worked with a variety of teams throughout my career, I've learned that these individuals often aren't rejecting ideas because they're flawed, they're rejecting them because they didn't come up with the idea themselves or because they feel the need to assert their opinions.

What's even more telling is that these "Yeah Butters" are often the least successful people in the group. Their focus on being right or maintaining control takes precedence over contributing meaningfully to a project. Instead of generating solutions or offering constructive feedback, they create friction. This isn't just unproductive, it's toxic. If you find yourself working with someone like this, my advice is simple: either avoid them altogether or, if that's not an option, take their input with a huge grain of salt.

Ultimately, collaboration is about building something better together, not tearing down ideas before they've had a chance to take root. Constructive criticism is valuable, but it's a world away from the knee-jerk negativity that defines the "Yeah Butter" mindset. Surround yourself with people who uplift, challenge, and inspire you, people who are focused on solutions, not problems. By doing so, you'll create an environment where innovation thrives and everyone has the opportunity to succeed.

Real-World Example: The Magic of a Shared Vision

Consider the group I've worked with for 26 years The Sam Morrison Band. Through the power of collaboration. Each member brings unique talents to the table, but it's the shared commitment to a common vision that keeps the band's sound and spirit alive. Whether recording an album, playing live, or brainstorming new ideas, the foundation of trust and mutual respect ensures every project shines.

This is a powerful example of the magic that unfolds when a shared vision guides a team. Over 25 years, we have thrived not just because of individual talent but through the synergy created by collaboration. Each member brings unique skills, perspectives, and creative energy to the table, but the unifying force is their unwavering commitment to a common goal: crafting music that resonates deeply with their audience. This shared purpose has been the backbone of their enduring success, enabling them to adapt, grow, and stay relevant in an ever-changing industry.

When recording an album or preparing for a live show, the band's dynamic is a testament to the power of trust and mutual respect. Every idea, whether a new riff, a lyrical concept, or a tweak in production, is given space to breathe and evolve within a supportive environment. The result is a sound that feels cohesive yet vibrant, reflecting the collective input of a group that values each member's contributions equally. This balance between individual creativity and collective harmony has allowed them to produce work that not only meets but often exceeds their shared expectations.

Beyond the music itself, The Sam Morrison Band exemplifies how a shared vision fosters a sense of family among collaborators. Brainstorming sessions, late-night rehearsals, and the challenges of life on the road become opportunities to strengthen their bond. The respect they have for one another ensures that creative differences are resolved constructively, allowing the band to remain focused on their ultimate goal. It's this unity of purpose that has kept their sound alive and vibrant for over two decades, inspiring fans and fellow musicians alike.

The Sam Morrison Band has seen its share of members come and go over the decades, a natural evolution for any group with such longevity. Despite these changes, the band has consistently retained its distinct sound and spirit, a testament to the unwavering vision of its core members. These founding figures have nurtured the band's identity with dedication, ensuring that every song, performance, and creative decision reflects their shared commitment to excellence. While new members have brought fresh perspectives and talents, the core vision acts as a guiding light, preventing the band from veering off course.

However, there have been times when new members have struggled to find their place within the band's dynamic. Some have entered the group with an overly assertive approach, immediately referring to it as "our band" or even "my band," despite being new to the team. While enthusiasm is valuable, this kind of behavior can feel disheartening to the long-standing members who have invested years of hard work and built the foundation of the band's success. Such actions can come across as pushy or even dismissive of the history and camaraderie that bind the original members together.

If you find yourself joining an established group, it's important to approach the opportunity with humility and respect for what has already been created. Take the time to understand the dynamics, learn the history, and earn your place as a valued contributor. Forcing your ideas or attempting to assert authority prematurely can alienate you from the group and undermine the very cohesion that drew you to the band in the first place. Instead, focus on building trust and proving your worth through your dedication and contributions.

For existing members, it's equally crucial not to rest on the laurels of others' efforts. Every member has a responsibility to actively contribute to the group's success, whether through creative input, logistical support, or fostering a positive team environment. Being an asset means consistently adding value and taking initiative while respecting the shared vision that defines the band. By maintaining this balance, both new and existing members can help ensure the group continues to thrive, preserving its unique identity for years to come.

Personal Relationships and Band Members

Relationships in the music business can be incredibly complex. On rare occasions, couples like Pat Benatar and Neil Giraldo have managed to forge successful careers while maintaining both their personal and professional partnerships. Their collaboration thrives because of mutual respect, clearly defined roles, and a shared passion for their art. However, such examples are the exception rather than the rule, and their success story often overshadows the challenges that most bands face when significant others are involved.

For bands starting out, it's often not the best idea to bring a significant other into the mix. While the intention might be to create a supportive environment, it can easily backfire. Many times, the non-musical partner can unintentionally disrupt the band's dynamics, sometimes coming across as overly involved or pushy. This can lead to tension and even resentment within the group. At worst, the significant other might be perceived as the "Yoko Ono" of the band, a reference to someone whose presence creates division rather than unity.

I've personally witnessed numerous instances where drama and tears arose unnecessarily due to such situations, making rehearsals, gigs, and tours uncomfortable for everyone involved. The added emotional strain can derail a band's focus on the music, which should always be the primary goal. While relationships and partnerships can bring joy and inspiration, they also require boundaries and careful management to avoid negatively impacting the collective vision and cohesion of the group.

This is a Special Forces Relationship

A good band member, like a soldier in the Navy SEALs or any elite special forces unit, is defined by more than just individual skill and proficiency. Yes, the technical abilities, mastering their instrument, knowing their gear, reading music, and learning songs quickly, are critical. But the true essence of a great band member lies in their ability to place the needs of the group above their own. This sense of unity and team-first mentality creates an environment where the band can thrive creatively and professionally, much

L to R: **Adam Parsons and Bart**

like how a special forces unit relies on mutual trust and shared purpose to accomplish its mission.

The analogy to elite military teams is particularly apt because both contexts demand an unwavering commitment to the team's success. In the SEALs, every member has a role, and the mission comes before personal gain or ego. Similarly, in a band, personal agendas must be set aside to serve the greater good of the group's music and goals. Ego clashes and selfish behavior can quickly unravel even the most talented ensembles. Bands break up more often due to interpersonal conflicts and selfishness than because of musical differences. A great band member knows that their personal ambitions are secondary to the collective goals of the group.

Another crucial quality is adaptability. In both bands and special forces units, situations can change rapidly, and the ability to adjust is key. Whether it's handling last-minute setlist changes, adapting to unexpected travel issues, or dealing with onstage technical problems, a good band member stays calm and focused. They don't point fingers or crumble under pressure; instead, they find solutions and support their team. This adaptability fosters resilience and ensures that the band can weather challenges together, strengthening their bond.

Communication is another pillar of what makes a good band member. Just as special forces teams rely on clear, concise communication to execute missions, a band thrives when its members communicate openly and respectfully. A good band member doesn't let resentment fester or avoid tough conversations. Instead, they address issues constructively, ensuring that conflicts are resolved in a way that reinforces the group's cohesion rather than tearing it apart.

Respect and mutual support are also critical. Great band members understand that every role in the group is vital. They respect the contributions of others, whether it's the guitarist's intricate riffs, the drummer's steady grooves, or the manager's hard work behind the scenes. This respect fosters a culture of appreciation, where everyone feels valued and motivated to give their best. It's the same in the military, where every team member is essential to the mission's success, from the sniper to the medic.

Ultimately, what makes a great band member is their dedication to the shared mission of creating and performing music that resonates with audiences. This requires humility, discipline, and a willingness to prioritize the band's success over personal glory. Just like in the military, it's not about being the hero; it's about being part of a team that achieves something greater together than any individual could alone. When every member adopts this mindset, the band becomes an unstoppable force.

Trust the Belief Others Have in You

In the music business, we're constantly surrounded by incredibly talented people. Whether it's during gigs, in the studio, or even scrolling through social media, it's easy to fall into the trap of comparison. You might find yourself thinking, "They're so much better than me," or, "I'll never measure up." These thoughts can quickly snowball into imposter syndrome, the persistent feeling that you're not good enough or that you don't belong, even when all evidence points to the contrary.

Here's the truth: when someone believes in you, it's for a reason. They see something in you that you might not be able to see in yourself. Maybe it's your unique style, your work ethic, your creativity, or your ability to connect with an audience. Whatever it is, their belief in you is real, and it's something to be trusted.

Imposter syndrome thrives on self-doubt. It's that inner critic that whispers (or sometimes shouts) that you're not good enough, that you're going to fail, or that you don't deserve the opportunities you've been given. But that inner critic is often a liar. Instead of listening to that voice, lean into the belief others have in you. It's a powerful antidote to self-doubt.

Think about the mentors, collaborators, or fans who have supported you. They've seen your potential and invested in you because they know you're capable of great things. Trust their perspective over the distorted view your inner critic provides. It's not arrogance to believe in yourself; it's honoring the faith others have placed in you.

When you find yourself doubting your abilities, remind yourself of the times you've succeeded, the hard work you've put in, and the people who've stood in your corner. Instead of letting imposter syndrome hold you back, use it as a signal to push forward. Remember, no one achieves success alone. Those who believe in you are part of your journey, and their faith in you can help carry you through moments of doubt.

In this business, there will always be someone more skilled, more experienced, or more successful. But that doesn't diminish your worth or your unique contributions. The world doesn't need another copy of someone else; it needs what only you can offer. So the next time someone expresses their belief in you, trust it. Use it as fuel to keep going, even when the road feels uncertain. Their faith in you is a gift, accept it, embrace it, and let it remind you of the greatness you're capable of achieving.

Time To Let This One Go

Working in a band is often like being in a marriage, the dynamic is deeply personal, and the success of the group relies on mutual respect, shared goals, and communication. But sometimes, the best decision you can make for yourself and your career is to let a working relationship go, no matter how long it's lasted or how much history you share. I learned this the hard way after a 20-year working relationship with a guitarist who became one of the most toxic people I've ever encountered.

For the better part of two decades, we shared stages, recorded albums, logged thousands of miles on the road, and were roommates while on tour. We weathered the ups and downs of the music business together no matter what. At first, it was a dream collaboration. We had chemistry, we inspired each other creatively, and we both worked hard to build something bigger than ourselves. But over time, the cracks began to show. What once seemed like passion for his craft began to reveal itself as a deep-seated arrogance. Constructive criticism turned into personal attacks, and minor disagreements became full-blown conflicts.

The breaking point came when his toxicity started to affect not just me but every aspect of the band. Rehearsals became hostile, and gigs felt like walking on eggshells, He refused to take responsibility for his actions, and instead of addressing the issues at hand, he pointed fingers. The moment he walked away from our working relationship, there was no apology, no accountability. He just bailed and left us hanging at a gig. It was painful but also a profound lesson in recognizing when enough is enough.

His departure, however, awoke a sleeping giant inside me. Before he left, he once told me, "You're not a songwriter." Those words stuck with me and fueled the "D", "Determination" in me kicked into overdrive.

Since then, I teamed up with two amazing songwriting partners, Blackthorne and Todd McTavish. We've written and recorded two albums under the banner of The Runs, one of which, Scavenger, is about this very situation. We've had the privilege of collaborating with two amazing and extremely successful guitar players, Jeff Duncan and Stevie Dacanay. I built a recording studio from the ground up, creating a space to nurture creativity and innovation. Beyond music, I've authored two books, each one a testament to the resilience and growth that came from leaving that toxic relationship behind.

Sometimes, letting go of a long-standing relationship feels like admitting defeat. But in reality, it's an act of self-preservation and an investment in your future. No matter how much history you have with someone, you can't allow their behavior to sabotage your happiness, creativity, or professionalism. Walking away from that partnership was one of the hardest things I've ever been through, but it was also one of the most liberating. It gave me the space to refocus, heal, and surround myself with people who uplift rather than undermine.

In the end, every working relationship, like every song, has its own tempo, it's rhythm and feel. When the harmony is gone and all that remains is discord, it's time to close the book on that chapter. Letting go doesn't mean forgetting the good times or erasing the past; it means making room for something better, something healthier, and something that aligns with your vision for the future.

Wherever You Go, There You Are

One of the most important relationships you'll ever have is the one with yourself. Being real with yourself means acknowledging both your strengths and your weaknesses. For me, my strengths lie in my resilience and creativity. I've always had the ability to push through challenges, whether it's learning a new skill, facing rejection, or navigating difficult relationships. My creative drive has been a constant source of renewal and purpose, helping me express myself through music, writing, and collaborations. But strengths don't exist in a vacuum; they're often accompanied by blind spots or vulnerabilities that can hold us back if left unchecked.

One of my weaknesses is an over-reliance on perfectionism. I've spent years chasing the illusion of getting everything just right, whether it's a drum track, a song mix, or even the way I approach personal growth. While striving for excellence can be a good thing, it's also a trap that can leave you feeling paralyzed or perpetually dissatisfied. Another challenge I've faced is learning how to trust myself, truly trust my instincts and decisions without second-guessing or seeking constant external validation. It's a work in progress, but I've found that leaning into self-awareness has helped me take steps toward genuine confidence.

Being honest with yourself also means looking at the areas of your life where you might need help. Addiction is a tough subject, but it's one I've had to confront head-on. Whether it's an unhealthy reliance on substances, distractions, or negative thought patterns, recognizing when you're stuck in a destructive cycle is the first step toward change. Recovery isn't linear, and it's not something you have to tackle alone. I've leaned on friends, family, and professional resources to work through these issues, and I've learned that asking for help is a sign of strength, not weakness.

At the end of the day, the relationship you have with yourself sets the tone for everything else in your life. If you're not taking care of your physical and mental well-being, it's nearly impossible to show up fully for others or your craft. Learning to love yourself, warts and all is a lifelong journey. But it's a journey worth taking because wherever you go, there you are. The better you know and nurture yourself, the more equipped you'll be to navigate whatever life throws your way.

In the music business, relationships are the rhythm that keeps everything moving forward. By networking with purpose, cultivating meaningful connections, and building trust, you lay the groundwork for a thriving career. And when you embrace collaboration, you create something far greater than the sum of its parts. Remember, it's not just about who you know; it's about how you nurture those relationships that make all the difference.

Just as in music, where a steady rhythm holds the entire composition together, purposeful networking forms the foundation of a successful career. Building connections with intention, not simply for personal gain but to foster mutual growth and opportunity, ensures that your professional network is both vibrant and enduring. Each conversation, shared experience, and collaboration becomes a note in the symphony of your career, harmonizing with others to create something powerful and lasting.

Cultivating meaningful connections and building trust takes time and effort but is well worth the investment. Genuine relationships are not transactional; they thrive on authenticity, reciprocity, and a willingness to help others succeed. When you prioritize these values, you create a network of allies who not only support your goals but also inspire you to grow and achieve new heights. Trust, once established, becomes the glue that holds these relationships together, enabling collaboration and innovation to flourish in ways that would be impossible alone.

Ultimately, collaboration is the key to creating something greater than the sum of its parts. In business, as in music, the most remarkable achievements often come from blending diverse talents, ideas, and perspectives. It's not merely about who you know but how you nurture those relationships that truly make a difference. By approaching every interaction with respect, and a shared vision, you can transform simple connections into meaningful partnerships that amplify your impact and pave the way for a thriving career.

Chapter 3:
U - Understanding: The Key to Growth

In the music industry, success is rarely a straight line. It's a journey with twists, turns, and unexpected detours. To navigate this path effectively, you need a deep understanding of not only your craft but also yourself, the industry, and the steps required to achieve your goals. Understanding is your compass, guiding you toward success.

Understanding is the cornerstone of growth in any field, and the music business is no exception. In this chapter, we'll explore how mastering the art of understanding can pave the way for success. This involves not only knowing your market and audience but also developing emotional intelligence, embracing change, analyzing feedback, and deepening your understanding of your instrument, business, and everything in between.

Understand Your Instrument

First and foremost, you must understand your instrument. Whether you're a drummer, guitarist, vocalist, or any other type of musician, your instrument is the vehicle for your creativity. Dive deep into its nuances. Explore different techniques and sounds. Experiment with styles that push you out of your comfort zone. The more you understand your instrument, the better equipped you'll be to adapt to various musical situations.

For drummers, this might mean mastering not just rock grooves but also jazz, funk, Latin, and other genres. A well-rounded skill set opens doors you might not have considered. The session that starts with a rock beat could evolve into a samba breakdown, you never know. Being versatile makes you an asset to any project.

Deepening Understanding Across the Board

Growth isn't just about becoming a better musician; it's about becoming a well-rounded professional. Here are the areas to focus on:

- **Your instrument:** *Invest time in mastering your primary instrument and exploring new techniques and styles. Understand its history and versatility.*

- **Musical styles:** *Study different genres to diversify your skills and increase your versatility.*

- **The business:** *Learn the basics of contracts, royalties, copyright, and licensing. This knowledge will protect you and open doors to new opportunities.*

- **Social media:** *Develop an understanding of how to use social media effectively. Learn about algorithms, engagement strategies, and branding.*

- **Networking:** *Build relationships with other musicians, producers, and industry professionals. Understanding how to connect meaningfully with others can lead to collaborations and opportunities.*

Understand the Styles

- **Musical styles:** *Study different genres to diversify your skills and increase your versatility.*

Understanding different musical styles is equally important. The music industry is a melting pot of genres, and being fluent in multiple styles will significantly expand your opportunities. Study the legends of each genre. Listen carefully to the nuances that make a jazz ride cymbal pattern different from a swing shuffle or a hip-hop backbeat. Embrace the challenge of learning something new, it's one of the most rewarding aspects of being a musician.

Understand the Business

- **The business:** *Learn the basics of contracts, royalties, copyright, and licensing. This knowledge will protect you and open doors to new opportunities.*

This book is called Drum Up Your Business for a reason. To thrive as a musician, you must understand the business side of the industry. It's not enough to be talented; you need to know how to market yourself, network effectively, and manage your career.

Understanding the business starts with recognizing that your music is a product, and you are a brand. How do you present yourself? Do you have a professional website and social media presence? Are you reaching out to venues, producers, or collaborators? These are the actions that propel a career forward.

More importantly, understand that no one will hand you success. If you're sitting at home waiting for the phone to ring, it's not going to happen. It's up to you to make things happen. Whether it's booking gigs, reaching out to industry professionals, or creating content to showcase your talent, the daily push forward is what fans the flames of success.

The Importance of Understanding Branding

In today's competitive world, whether you're a musician, entrepreneur, or business owner, understanding branding is a critical part of your success. Branding is not just about your name; it's about creating a unique identity that resonates with your audience. At the heart of this identity is your logo, a visual symbol that represents who you are and what you stand for.

Why Your Logo Matters

Your logo is often the first thing people see when they encounter your brand. It's your calling card, your signature, and a powerful visual cue that leaves a lasting impression. Iconic logos like the electrifying Kiss logo or the unmistakable Rolling Stones lips are more than just designs; they are symbols of the energy, attitude, and legacy these bands represent. Their logos are instantly recognizable, transcending language and geography, and they've become synonymous with their respective brands.

A strong logo communicates your essence at a glance. It tells your story, evokes emotion, and establishes your brand's credibility. When designed and used effectively, your logo becomes an anchor for all your branding efforts, tying together your merchandise, online presence, and promotional materials.

Making Your Mark

Creating your own logo is an essential step in establishing your brand. A well-designed logo should be:

L to R: **DEC - Jeremy Steinkoler, Rick Stojak and Bart at PASIC 2024**

- **Simple:** *Easy to recognize and remember.*
- **Relevant:** *Reflective of your values and mission.*
- **Versatile:** *Suitable for use across various mediums, from social media profiles to merchandise.*
- **Timeless:** *Avoid trends that may fade; aim for a design that will remain relevant for years.*

Once you've developed your logo, use it consistently. Place it on everything you do: your website, business cards, stage backdrop, merchandise, and social media platforms. Consistency reinforces recognition, which builds trust and loyalty with your audience. Here is a copy of my logo, which was created years ago, and I make sure it's on everything I do.

Studying Iconic Logos

To truly appreciate the power of a logo, take the time to study some of the most successful ones:

- **Kiss:** *The angular, bold design of their logo captures the band's edgy and rebellious spirit.*

- **The Rolling Stones:** *The iconic lips and tongue graphic, designed by John Pasche, perfectly embodies the band's sensual and provocative rock 'n' roll image.*

- **Nike:** *The simple swoosh conveys movement and speed, aligning with the brand's focus on athleticism and innovation.*

These logos aren't just designs; they're the visual shorthand for entire cultural movements, encapsulating the essence of their brands in a single glance.

Your Logo, Your Legacy

By creating and consistently using your own logo, you're not just branding your work–you're building your legacy. Your logo becomes a rallying point for your fans, clients, and supporters, a symbol that they'll proudly associate with your artistry, products, or services. Invest time and thought into this vital piece of your branding puzzle, and let it be a beacon that guides your audience to you.

Remember, a great logo is more than an image; it's a promise. Make it bold. Make it memorable. Make it yours.

Understand Your Dreams

Understanding also extends to your dreams. The vision you have for your career today might look different once you achieve it. That's not a bad thing; it's a sign of growth. Dreams evolve as you gain experience and clarity. Be open to the idea that your path might take you in a direction you hadn't expected. For example, you might start out wanting to be a touring musician and end up discovering a passion for teaching or producing.

What's important is that you're actively working toward your dream. Understand that success requires effort every single day. If you're spending more time at the beach or Disneyland than in your practice space or studio, your dream will remain just that, a dream. Success doesn't come looking for you; you have to chase it with determination and discipline.

- **Self-awareness:** *Recognize your strengths and weaknesses to make informed decisions about your career.*

Self-awareness is the foundation of personal and professional growth. By understanding your strengths, you can leverage them to stand out in a competitive market. For example, if you excel in live performances, you might focus on building a reputation as a dynamic stage presence. Conversely, knowing your weaknesses allows you to address them head-on. Whether it's improving your technical skills, enhancing your marketing efforts, or learning more about the business side of music, self-awareness guides your priorities.

Recognizing your limitations doesn't mean dwelling on them; it means taking proactive steps to grow. For instance, if you struggle with networking, you might attend workshops or seek mentorship to build confidence in social settings. Self-awareness helps you identify opportunities for improvement, turning potential roadblocks into stepping stones for success.

Ultimately, self-awareness fosters authenticity. When you understand and embrace who you are as an artist, you can create music and cultivate a brand that genuinely reflects your identity. This authenticity resonates with audiences and industry professionals alike, building trust and deepening connections that can propel your career forward.

Take Responsibility for Your Career

Ultimately, you're responsible for your own career. There are no shortcuts, no magic formulas. It's about showing up every day, putting in the work, and staying focused on your goals. The music industry is competitive, but there's room for those who are prepared and persistent.

Understand that setbacks are part of the journey. You might not land every gig or secure every opportunity you pursue. That's okay. Each experience, good or bad, teaches you something valuable. The key is to keep moving forward and keep fanning the flames of success.

Understand No One Is Waiting On You

In the music business, it's easy to fall into the trap of waiting for the right moment or relying on someone else to take action for you. We've all heard the stories from musicians who claim that a record label is waiting on their next album or a publisher is eager to sign their book deal. The truth, however, is that no one is waiting for you to make your move, time doesn't wait for anyone. In the fast-paced world of music, opportunities don't simply knock on your door; you have to go out and create them yourself. You need to take charge of your career, make the calls, and take the necessary actions to move things forward.

Rather than waiting for others to take the initiative, it's essential to be proactive. If you want to get your album recorded and into the hands of your fans, it's up to you to find the right studio, gather the resources, and dedicate the time and effort to make it happen. No record label is going to magically show up at your doorstep to sign you, if you have a great product, you need to take the steps to get it out there, promote it, and build your fanbase. The same goes for any other project in the music business. You can't wait for someone to tell you it's time to write that book or release your next single. You need to take the reins and drive the process.

The reality is, that if your work is good enough, others will notice. Whether it's a record label, publisher, or booking agent, they are always looking for the next successful project. But they're not going to chase you down; you need to put in the work and prove that you have something valuable to offer. You need to build a reputation, develop your craft, and put yourself out there. If you wait for the right person to come to you, you may be waiting a long time. But if you make the effort to actively pursue your goals, others will take notice and will want to work with you.

If you want to see results, you have to be relentless in your determination. Making things happen in the music business requires persistence and resilience because success rarely comes easily. The difference between musicians who succeed and those who don't often boils down to who is willing to put in the hard work and take risks. It's easy to get discouraged when things don't happen right away, but that's when your drive and commitment to follow through will make all the difference. You may encounter setbacks, but the key is to keep moving forward and keep working, even when the progress feels slow.

Ultimately, the music business is about ownership and responsibility. You are the one who holds the keys to your success. If you want your music, your book, or your project to be seen and heard, you have to take action. It's easy to assume someone will come along and offer you the opportunity, but that's not how it works. The most successful musicians and creatives are the ones who create opportunities for themselves, build their own paths, and keep pushing forward with determination. You need to make it happen because no one else will.

Emotional Intelligence in the Music Business

The music business is as much about relationships as it is about talent. Emotional intelligence can be your superpower. It's the ability to recognize, understand, and manage your own emotions while empathizing with others.

- **Empathy:** *Understanding the needs and emotions of collaborators, fans, and industry professionals can help you build lasting connections.*

Empathy is the bridge that connects you to the people who shape your career. By putting yourself in the shoes of collaborators, you can better understand their creative vision and find ways to complement it, leading to a stronger partnership. For fans, empathy means recognizing their desires and emotional responses to your music, which can inspire deeper loyalty and engagement. When it comes to industry professionals, understanding their goals and pressures can foster mutual respect and lead to more fruitful collaborations. Empathy is not just about listening; it's about responding thoughtfully and creating meaningful relationships that endure over time.

- **Conflict resolution:** *Disagreements are inevitable, but handling them gracefully can set you apart as a professional.*

Conflict resolution is an essential skill in the music business, where creative passions and differing perspectives often intersect. Disagreements with collaborators, band members, or industry professionals are bound to arise, but your ability to handle these situations with poise can elevate your reputation. Begin by addressing conflicts with an open mind and a willingness to listen. Acknowledging the perspectives of others not only demonstrates respect but also fosters an environment where solutions can be collaboratively explored.

Effective communication is the cornerstone of resolving conflicts gracefully. Clearly articulate your concerns and needs while remaining receptive to the input of others. Strive to maintain a professional tone, even in emotionally charged situations, as this can de-escalate tension and pave the way for productive dialogue. Compromise, when appropriate, can also be a powerful tool, as it shows your commitment to finding a resolution that benefits all parties involved.

Lastly, view conflicts as opportunities for growth rather than obstacles. Each disagreement you navigate successfully strengthens your interpersonal skills and deepens your understanding of working relationships. By handling conflicts with grace and professionalism, you not only resolve immediate issues but also build a reputation as someone who can thrive in collaborative and high-pressure environments. This reputation can open doors to new opportunities and solidify long-term partnerships.

Understanding Multiple Income Streams as a Professional Musician

Being a professional drummer or musician is a dynamic and rewarding career, but it requires a deep understanding of the realities of income in the music industry. Even if you're in a touring band, particularly as a side musician, the financial flow is not constant. Once the tour ends, you're essentially unemployed until the next opportunity arises. This ebb and flow makes it critical to establish multiple streams of income that can sustain you between gigs and over the long term. The myth of perpetual stardom is far from reality for most musicians, so diversification is the key to stability and growth.

One of the most accessible ways to create additional income is through education. Teaching private lessons, conducting masterclasses, or hosting clinics allows you to share your expertise while building a steady income stream. Writing instructional books, contributing columns to industry websites or print magazines, and offering online courses are other avenues that not only generate revenue but also establish you as a thought leader in your field. These activities deepen your connection to the music community and broaden your career opportunities beyond the stage.

Another lucrative path is developing and selling products. Perhaps you've invented a drumming accessory or have the means to invest in an innovative product. Launching a home studio for session work is another excellent way to keep your schedule full and your wallet steady. With the increasing accessibility of recording technology, many drummers are offering high-quality remote session work to artists worldwide. The ability to track drums from your studio allows you to work with clients across genres, keeping your skills sharp and your creative output high.

Even at the top of the game, musicians often pursue side ventures to maintain their careers and personal growth. Look at industry veterans: while they may headline stadium tours or record with legendary artists, they're often involved in writing, producing, or endorsing products on the side. Understanding that the limelight is not a guaranteed or everlasting source of income is crucial. The more diversified your skill set and income streams, the more resilient and successful you'll be in navigating the challenges of the music business.

Understand What Not To Do

It's easy to romanticize the wild antics of bands like Mötley Crüe, who built their reputation on being an obnoxious group of alcohol-fueled, sex-crazed maniacs. For them, that behavior was not only expected but became a part of their brand. However, let's be real, you're not in Mötley Crüe. Acting out in similar ways is not something any promoter, agent, manager, or casino buyer will tolerate. If you want to build a sustainable career in music, professionalism is key.

The music industry has long been plagued by addiction, and it's important to recognize when help is needed. As of the writing of this book, I've been sober for six years. I can personally attest to the fact that acting like an asshole will only drive you down and leave a trail of destruction behind you. This path is neither fulfilling nor something you'll look back on with pride. If you're struggling with addiction, don't hesitate to seek support, your career and well-being depend on it.

There are exceptions to every rule, but betting on being the exception is a gamble that rarely pays off. While some people manage to survive their reckless behavior and even thrive, most don't. It's far better to cultivate a reputation as a reliable, professional musician than to become another cautionary tale. Respect the people you work with, take care of yourself, and remember that the music should always come first.

Ultimately, your goal should be to leave a positive impression on everyone you encounter in the industry. The stories of rock-and-roll excess may be entertaining, but they're not a roadmap for success. Treat your career with the seriousness it deserves, and you'll find that professionalism opens far more doors than self-destructive behavior ever could.

Understand You Have To Make It Happen

Have you ever heard the old saying, "It's not the size of the dog in the fight, it's the size of the fight in the dog"? Let me clarify: I'm not advocating dog fighting but rather emphasizing the mindset needed to tackle life's challenges. Anything worthwhile in life requires effort, and the music business is no exception. Whether you're trying to land gigs, book studio sessions, or promote your latest single, the work often falls squarely on your shoulders. It can feel like you're climbing an endless hill, but remember, persistence is key.

In the music industry, there's rarely a straightforward path to success. You'll face rejection, unexpected obstacles, and moments of doubt. These challenges can be disheartening, but they're also opportunities to learn, grow, and build resilience. When things get tough, lean into the determination that got you started in the first place. Remind yourself that every successful artist, producer, and songwriter once faced the same uphill battle. Their perseverance is what sets them apart.

One way to keep your energy up during these moments is to reflect on your love of music. Think back to the first time you picked up an instrument or wrote your first song. Reconnect with the joy and passion that inspired you to pursue this path. This reflection isn't just about nostalgia; it's about grounding yourself in your purpose. That sense of connection can be a powerful motivator when everything feels overwhelming.

Finally, remember to celebrate small wins along the way. Did you book a show, gain a new fan, or finish recording a track? Those moments matter, and they're proof that your hard work is paying off. Success in music isn't about overnight achievements; it's about steady progress and the willingness to fight for your dreams. Keep pushing forward, and don't forget that the journey itself is part of the reward.

Understand It's Not All About You

In the music business, it can be tempting to believe that your talent or contribution is the most important piece of the puzzle. However, success in this industry requires recognizing that you are part of a larger ecosystem. Whether you're in a band, working on a session, or collaborating on a project, it's essential to "play nice with the other kids in the playground." This means respecting the roles, talents, and perspectives of others while finding your place within the group dynamic. True collaboration requires humility and a willingness to see the bigger picture.

Start by asking yourself tough but necessary questions: Are you pulling your weight? This means being prepared, showing up on time, and delivering your best performance every time. If you're not adequately contributing, you're not just letting yourself down–you're letting down everyone who is counting on you. Professionalism is a cornerstone of understanding your role in a team. It's not enough to be good at what you do; you must also be dependable and proactive in ensuring the team's success.

Conversely, it's possible to push too hard, which can disrupt the harmony of the group. Are you trying to dominate rehearsals, insisting on your way, or undervaluing others' input? This kind of behavior can erode trust and create tension, ultimately hindering the creative process. Collaboration thrives on balance, and being overly aggressive can stifle others' creativity. Remember, the best music comes from a place of mutual respect and shared vision.

At the same time, ask yourself if you're not pushing hard enough. Are you holding back ideas or not contributing because you're afraid of stepping on toes? Collaboration requires courage as much as restraint. If you have a valuable perspective or idea, share it constructively. The key is to contribute in a way that uplifts the group rather than detracting from it. Being passive in a team setting can lead to missed opportunities and a sense of dissatisfaction for everyone involved.

Ultimately, understanding that it's not all about you is about fostering an environment where everyone feels heard, valued, and empowered to bring their best. When you learn to balance your individual drive with the needs of the group, you set the stage for true harmony, both musically and professionally. Success in the music business, as in life, is rarely a solo endeavor. It's a collaborative symphony where every instrument plays a part in creating something extraordinary.

Bart and Jeff Kelly

Understanding Is the Foundation

Understanding is not a one-time achievement but a continuous journey. The more you understand about your market, audience, instrument, and the ever-changing landscape of the music business, the more equipped you'll be to navigate challenges and seize opportunities. With every step, your growth will reflect your commitment to becoming not just a better musician, but a true professional in the music industry.

Understanding is the foundation upon which you'll build your career. It encompasses your instrument, the styles you play, the business you navigate, and the dreams you chase. By cultivating a deep understanding of these elements, you'll be better equipped to turn your passion for music into a thriving career. Remember, success is a daily push forward. Keep your eyes on the horizon and your hands on the wheel, the journey is yours to take.

Chapter 4
Mentorship: Guiding Lights on the Path to Success

Mentorship is the backbone of growth in any industry, and in the music business, it's no different. The letter "M" in the acronym DRUM stands for mentorship, a key component in not just building your career but sustaining it over the long term. Whether you're the mentor or the mentee, this relationship is one of mutual benefit and immense value.

The Power of Mentorship

At its core, mentorship is about guidance, inspiration, and connection. A mentor shares their expertise and experience to help a mentee navigate the often challenging and unpredictable world of music. This could mean offering advice on honing your craft, managing the business side of things, or simply providing encouragement when the going gets tough.

A good mentor doesn't just tell you what to do; they help you think critically, make informed decisions, and avoid common pitfalls. They're like a compass, pointing you toward your true north while allowing you the freedom to chart your unique course.

Finding the Right Mentor

Not all mentors are created equal, and finding the right one requires intention and effort. Here are some tips to identify and connect with a mentor who aligns with your goals:

1. **Define Your Needs:** *What aspects of your career do you need guidance on? Are you looking for musical/technical skills, business insights, or emotional support? Don't underestimate emotional support in the music business. Anything artistic touches our ego, and the pressures of performing, creating, and navigating a competitive industry can take a toll. A mentor who understands this dynamic can provide invaluable encouragement and help you build resilience in the face of criticism or setbacks.*

Expand your self-awareness by asking yourself tough questions. Do you struggle with stage fright, imposter syndrome, or the emotional highs and lows of a creative life? A mentor can help you work through these challenges, offering both practical advice and emotional grounding. Sometimes, just knowing that someone else has faced similar struggles and come out stronger can be the support you need to keep pushing forward.

It's also important to remember that emotional support isn't about coddling; it's about empowerment. A mentor who genuinely believes in your potential can help you develop the confidence to take risks and learn from your failures. Their encouragement can serve as a reminder that you're not alone in your journey, providing a sense of community and camaraderie that's vital for long-term success.

Mentorship in Action

I've been fortunate to have incredible mentors throughout my career, individuals who pushed me to refine my drumming skills, understand the music business and become a better educator. One of my earliest mentors taught me the importance of preparation, showing up to every gig, session, or rehearsal, ready to give my best.

On the flip side, I've mentored countless students and colleagues, sharing what I've learned over three decades in the industry. Watching someone I've mentored achieve their goals is one of the most rewarding aspects of my career. It's a reminder that success is never a solo endeavor.

Take Dom Famularo, for example. Known as "Drumming's Global Ambassador," Dom dedicated his life not only to mastering the drums but also to inspiring countless drummers worldwide. His infectious energy, love for teaching, and commitment to spreading positivity made him a pillar in the drumming community. Whether through his books, clinics, or one-on-one lessons, Dom's mission was clear: to empower drummers to find their voice and share it with the world. His influence continues to resonate globally, proving that mentorship extends far beyond any single lesson or performance.

Similarly, Jim Chapin, often regarded as one of the greatest drum educators in history, left an indelible mark on the drumming world. His groundbreaking book, Advanced Techniques for the Modern Drummer, is a testament to his dedication to education. But it wasn't just his technical expertise that made him a great mentor—it was his passion for helping others achieve their potential. Jim's work laid the foundation for generations of drummers, and his influence can still be felt in drum studios and practice rooms around the globe.

Freddie Gruber was another extraordinary mentor who changed the lives of countless drummers, including legends like Neil Peart and Dave Weckl. Freddie's approach to drumming was as much about philosophy and movement as it was about technique. He encouraged his students to view drumming as a holistic art form, one that integrates body, mind, and spirit. His teachings didn't just make drummers better at their craft; they made them better artists and, often, better people.

Gregg Bissonette is yet another shining example of mentorship in action. Gregg has not only played for the biggest names in the business, David Lee Roth, Ringo Starr, and His All-Star Band, to name two, Gregg is known for his incredible versatility and joyful approach to drumming, Gregg has inspired drummers of all ages through his clinics, masterclasses, and performances. His willingness to share his experiences, both triumphs and challenges, makes him a relatable and impactful teacher. Gregg's mentorship has touched countless lives, proving that success is sweeter when shared.

2. **Seek Experience:** *Look for someone who has walked the path you're trying to tread. Their experiences, both good and bad, will provide valuable lessons. I've been in the music business my entire adult life. I've been there, done that, and bought the T-shirt. Over the years, I've learned that sharing these experiences, the triumphs, and the failures, is one of the most impactful ways to guide others. Each success story comes with lessons about perseverance and strategy, and each setback offers wisdom on resilience and adaptation.*

Life experience brings depth and authenticity to mentorship. It's not just about teaching technical skills but also about imparting real-world insights that go beyond the classroom or rehearsal space. For example, understanding the importance of networking, handling rejection, or navigating the complexities of contracts can only come from firsthand experience. I strive to pass this wealth of knowledge to each of my clients, ensuring they're better prepared for the realities of the industry.

I firmly believe that life experience is invaluable to music lessons and mentorship. The nuances of the music business, from managing tour schedules to dealing with creative blocks, cannot be fully understood through textbooks or tutorials alone. A mentor who has lived these experiences can provide actionable advice and relatable stories, making the guidance both practical and inspiring. By sharing my journey, I hope to equip others with the tools they need to succeed and the confidence to carve out their own paths.

> **3. Build Relationships:** *Mentorship often grows out of organic relationships. Attend industry events, join professional groups, and connect with people you admire. Show genuine interest in their work and let the relationship evolve naturally. Relationships are the lifeblood of the music business, a concept we explored in depth in the Relationships chapter. Whether it's building connections with fellow musicians, industry professionals, or potential mentors, fostering genuine relationships is essential to career growth.*

When you show interest in someone's work, it's more than just a compliment; it's an opportunity to learn and establish rapport. Attend workshops, conventions, or jam sessions, and don't be afraid to introduce yourself and strike up a conversation. Authenticity is key here. People can sense when your intentions are genuine, and this sincerity often paves the way for deeper connections.

Remember, mentorship relationships often take time to develop. They're built on trust, mutual respect, and a shared passion for music. Be patient and allow the relationship to grow naturally. Over time, these connections can evolve into mentorships that are not only valuable but also deeply fulfilling for both parties. The importance of these relationships cannot be overstated; they're the foundation upon which successful careers are built.

> **4. Be Proactive:** *Don't be afraid to ask someone to mentor you. Most people are flattered by the request and willing to share their knowledge if approached respectfully. Taking the initiative to ask for mentorship can feel intimidating, but it's a crucial step in your growth. Many seasoned professionals are eager to share their knowledge, and your genuine interest in their expertise will often resonate with them. Be clear about why you're seeking their guidance and what you hope to learn. When you approach someone with respect and humility, you're more likely to receive a positive response.*

Being proactive also means doing your homework. Before reaching out, learn about the person's career, achievements, and areas of expertise. Tailor your approach to demonstrate that you've taken the time to understand their journey. For example, if you admire their skill in session work or their ability to manage a successful band, mention these specific attributes. Showing that you've done your research not only flatters the potential mentor but also signals your seriousness and commitment.

Remember that mentorship is a two-way street. While you're seeking guidance, consider what you can offer in return, even if it's simply enthusiasm, fresh perspectives, or gratitude. Acknowledging the value of their time and effort strengthens the relationship. Proactive mentees who are eager to learn and willing to invest in the relationship often leave a lasting impression, creating a dynamic where both parties benefit and grow together.

The Mentor's Perspective

If you're in a position to mentor others, embrace the opportunity. Mentorship isn't just about giving; it's a two-way street. By sharing your knowledge, you'll often gain fresh perspectives and ideas from your mentees.

Here's how to be an effective mentor:

1. **Listen Actively:** *Understand your mentee's goals, challenges, and aspirations.*

Being a mentor is a profound responsibility that begins with active listening. This means more than simply hearing words; it requires a genuine effort to understand your mentee's goals, challenges, and aspirations. Active listening involves being fully present, free from distractions, and maintaining eye contact to show engagement. By doing so, mentors can create a safe space where mentees feel valued and confident enough to share their ambitions and vulnerabilities. The insight gained from listening allows mentors to tailor their guidance to the mentee's unique needs, fostering a relationship built on trust and mutual respect.

Understanding your mentee's goals requires delving into what truly motivates them. As a mentor, asking open-ended questions encourages your mentee to articulate their dreams and long-term objectives. This can lead to meaningful conversations that clarify the steps they need to take to achieve success. Equally important is recognizing their challenges and roadblocks. Listening actively enables a mentor to identify these obstacles, whether they are skill gaps, external pressures, or internal doubts, and helps the mentee develop strategies to overcome them.

Aspirations often reveal a mentee's deeper passions and values. Listening closely to these desires not only shows empathy but also helps a mentor align their advice to resonate with the mentee's personal vision of success. This alignment fosters motivation and commitment, as mentees see their mentor as someone who genuinely supports their journey. Moreover, by understanding aspirations, mentors can introduce resources, opportunities, or networks that might have otherwise been overlooked.

Ultimately, active listening is the foundation for meaningful mentorship. It goes beyond giving advice to truly understanding what drives and challenges a mentee. By being attentive and empathetic, mentors can inspire confidence, empower their mentees to overcome obstacles, and guide them toward their goals with clarity and purpose. This approach not only benefits the mentee but also enriches the mentor, as they witness the growth and success of the individual they have supported.

2. **Be Honest:** *Offer constructive feedback and share your own failures as learning opportunities.*

Honesty is one of the most critical qualities of a mentor, this is a BIG ONE! Offering constructive feedback and sharing your own failures is a powerful way to help your mentee grow. Sugarcoating or avoiding tough conversations may feel easier, but it denies your mentee the chance to confront areas for improvement. Constructive feedback, delivered with care and clarity, gives them actionable insights to build upon, while your willingness to share your own missteps demonstrates vulnerability and authenticity. It shows that failure is not the end but a stepping stone to success.

After a lifetime in the music business, I can say with certainty that I have fallen many times and made a lot of mistakes. There were times I misjudged opportunities, over-committed, or underestimated the challenges ahead. Some of those failures were tough to face, but each one taught me something valuable. Sharing these experiences with mentees not only helps them avoid similar pitfalls but also reassures them that failure is a natural part of the journey. It's important for them to know that even those who achieve great success have stumbled many times along the way.

Success, I've learned, is often found at the bottom of a pile of mistakes. Each setback holds the potential to teach us something critical, whether it's about resilience, problem-solving, or simply the importance of preparation.

When I reflect on my own path, I can pinpoint failures that, in hindsight, became the catalysts for growth. Sharing these lessons with a mentee helps them see that mistakes are not dead ends but opportunities to learn and pivot. This mindset shift can be a game-changer, fostering perseverance and confidence in their own abilities.

When you share your failures, it also humanizes you in the eyes of your mentee. It breaks down the illusion of perfection and makes success seem more attainable. They realize that the challenges they face are not unique and that others, even those they admire, have had to overcome similar struggles. This honesty strengthens the mentor-mentee relationship, creating a deeper connection and trust. By showing them how you turned failure into progress, you empower them to do the same.

Honesty is the foundation of meaningful mentorship because it creates an environment where growth can thrive. Offering constructive feedback and sharing failures shows your mentee that success is about persistence, self-reflection, and the ability to adapt. It teaches them to view challenges not as barriers but as opportunities to learn and improve. Ultimately, your honesty not only guides them in their journey but also equips them with the mindset and resilience to navigate the unpredictable path ahead.

3. **Encourage Independence:** *While guidance is essential, encourage your mentee to think for themselves and develop their problem-solving skills.*

One of the most important roles of a mentor is to encourage independence in a mentee. While providing guidance and support is essential, it's equally important to resist the urge to give all the answers. A mentor's goal should not be to create dependency but to equip their mentee with the tools they need to think critically and solve problems on their own. By encouraging independence, you help your mentee build confidence and develop the skills they'll need to navigate challenges long after the mentorship ends.

Encouraging independence starts with asking questions instead of providing solutions. When a mentee comes to you with a challenge, guide them through the problem-solving process rather than solving it for them. Ask open-ended questions like, "What do you think is the best approach?" or "Have you considered other perspectives?" These prompts empower the mentee to reflect, analyze, and take ownership of their decisions. Over time, they will become more comfortable relying on their own judgment, which is essential for personal and professional growth.

It's also important to create a supportive environment where mistakes are seen as opportunities to learn rather than failures to avoid. By stepping back and allowing your mentee to make their own choices, even if they might not always be the best ones, you give them the chance to grow from real-world experience. Share your own stories of trial and error to emphasize that missteps are a natural and valuable part of the learning process. This approach fosters resilience and resourcefulness, two qualities that are vital for success in any field.

Ultimately, the role of a mentor is not to lead every step but to walk alongside your mentee as they find their own path. By encouraging independence, you help them develop a sense of accountability, creativity, and self-reliance. This not only strengthens their ability to solve problems but also empowers them to trust their instincts and make confident decisions. In doing so, you prepare them to thrive in their career and life, equipped with the skills and mindset to succeed on their own terms.

4. **Stay Committed:** *Consistency and availability are crucial. Your mentee should feel they can count on you.*

Commitment is the cornerstone of effective mentorship. As a mentor, staying consistent and available is crucial to building a relationship of trust and reliability. Your mentee should feel they can count on you, knowing that you are invested in their growth and success. This doesn't mean you have to be available 24/7, but it does mean establishing a dependable rhythm of communication and support. Whether it's regular check-ins, scheduled meetings, or simply being responsive when they reach out, consistency shows that you take your role seriously.

One of the most valuable aspects of commitment is the sense of stability it provides for your mentee. Knowing they have someone they can rely on during times of uncertainty can make all the difference. It creates a safe environment where they feel comfortable seeking advice, sharing concerns, or celebrating achievements. This sense of security fosters confidence and encourages open dialogue, allowing for a more meaningful and productive mentorship experience.

Commitment also means showing up fully during your interactions. When you're with your mentee, be present and focused, giving them your undivided attention. Avoid distractions and listen actively to what they're saying and even to what they're not saying. By doing so, you demonstrate

Andrew Shreve (Gretsch Artist Relations) **and Bart.**

that their time and development matter to you. This level of engagement not only strengthens your bond but also sets a powerful example of how to approach relationships and responsibilities with care and dedication.

There will be times when staying committed requires extra effort. Life gets busy, and other priorities may compete for your attention, but honoring your commitment to your mentee is essential. If unforeseen circumstances arise, communicate openly and reschedule as needed. Your transparency reinforces trust and shows that even when things don't go as planned, you're still reliable and respectful of their time. It's this consistency that makes a lasting impact, reminding your mentee that they are valued and supported.

Ultimately, staying committed as a mentor is about creating a foundation of trust, stability, and respect. It's about showing up, being dependable, and demonstrating that their growth is as important to you as it is to them. By remaining consistent and available, you not only guide your mentee through their current challenges but also teach them the value of commitment in their own personal and professional relationships. This lesson will stay with them long after the mentorship ends, shaping how they approach their goals and connections in the future.

Starting Your Own Teaching Business

Starting a small teaching business can be one of the most rewarding ways to share your passion and expertise while making a living. For me, teaching drums began as a "side hustle" in high school, a way to earn some extra cash while doing something I loved. Little did I know that those early lessons would evolve into a full-fledged career. The journey of watching students grow and develop not only as drummers but as individuals has been one of the most fulfilling aspects of my life.

One of the keys to starting a teaching business is to identify your unique value as an instructor. For me, it was my ability to make lessons engaging and tailored to each student's needs. Whether it was helping a beginner learn their first basic beat or guiding a more advanced student to master complex rhythms, I focused on creating a positive and encouraging learning environment. This approach not only helped my students progress but also built a reputation that brought in more clients through word of mouth.

Building a teaching business from scratch requires more than just technical skill; it requires entrepreneurial spirit. When I first started, I taught lessons in my parents' garage and relied on flyers and referrals to find students. Over time, I learned the importance of marketing, scheduling, and managing finances. Today, technology makes it easier than ever to promote your services through social media, websites, and online lesson platforms. Don't be afraid to experiment with different ways to attract and retain students.

Another rewarding aspect of teaching is the ability to watch your students grow. Over the years, I've had the privilege of seeing many of my students join bands, write music, and even pursue professional music careers. Knowing that I played a small part in their journey is incredibly gratifying. Teaching isn't just about imparting technical knowledge; it's about inspiring confidence, creativity, and a lifelong love of music.

If you're considering starting your own teaching business, my advice is simple: go for it. Start small, be patient, and remember that every student is an opportunity to make a difference. Whether you're teaching out of your home, a rented studio, or even online, the impact you can have is immeasurable. Sharing your passion for music is one of the greatest gifts you can give, and the rewards, both personal and professional, are endless.

Find The Author Inside You

Writing books, whether instructional or literary, or writing columns for industry websites and magazines (yes, magazines still exist) is a deeply rewarding process that allows you to share your knowledge, experiences, and passion with a broader audience. My first book, *The School of Hard Rocks*, was a labor of love that took me quite a long time to complete. As a first-time author, I encountered numerous challenges, from organizing my ideas to refining the content in a way that would resonate with readers. However, the journey was worth every moment, as it not only helped me grow as a musician and educator but also opened the door to exciting new opportunities.

One of the most significant outcomes of writing *The School of Hard Rocks* was the creation of a companion DVD by the same name. At the time, DVDs were still a popular medium, and producing one allowed me to bring the concepts from the book to life in a more interactive format. The process of creating the DVD was an entirely new learning experience, requiring collaboration with videographer and editor Trey Solberg. The effort paid off in spades when the DVD earned a Bronze Telly Award, a recognition that validated all the hard work and reinforced the value of sharing my insights with the drumming community.

The success of *The School of Hard Rocks* and its DVD inspired me to continue writing, leading to my next project, *Rockin' Poppin' Snare Drum*. This instructional book focused on snare drum techniques and exercises, providing drummers with practical tools to improve their playing. By this point, I had gained confidence in my ability to write and structure content effectively. Each book became a stepping stone, building on the lessons learned from previous projects and expanding my reach as an educator. Writing instructional books also deepened my understanding of my own craft, as breaking down concepts for others often leads to new insights.

Over the years, my passion for writing has continued to grow, and the list of my published works has expanded. Each project presents its own set of challenges and rewards, but the overarching goal remains the same: to inspire and educate others. Whether it's through books, videos, or live workshops, the act of sharing knowledge is profoundly fulfilling. It's also a way to give back to the drumming community which has given me so much throughout my career.

For anyone considering writing their own book, my advice is to start small and be patient with the process. Writing is as much about persistence as it is about creativity. The journey of creating The School of Hard Rocks taught me that even the most ambitious projects can be completed one step at a time. Along the way, you'll discover more about your craft, connect with others in meaningful ways, and leave a lasting impact on those who read your work. The rewards of writing are immeasurable, and the possibilities are endless.

These giants of the drumming world didn't just play their instruments; they used their platforms to uplift others. Their mentorship has created ripples that extend far beyond their immediate students, impacting the global drumming community in ways that will be felt for generations. This is the power of passing on what you know in a loving and positive way.

As musicians, it's up to us to follow in their footsteps. Whether you're teaching a young student their first paradiddle, sharing your insights in a clinic, or simply encouraging a fellow musician who's struggling, every act of mentorship matters. You never know how your words, actions, or example might inspire someone to keep going, to push themselves further, or to fall in love with music all over again. Let's embrace our responsibility to nurture the next generation of musicians with the same generosity and passion as those who mentored us. In doing so, we ensure that the music, and the spirit of community it creates, will continue to thrive.

Before you tell yourself, "I could never write a book or a column," recognize that this is just an excuse. And when it comes to excuses, let me tell you, I've got a go-to one that's as big and juicy as they come: I have dyslexia. I was diagnosed in the first or second grade, and to make matters more challenging, I'm also a terrible speller, those two seem to go hand in hand. Even writing a short Facebook post can be agonizing. These challenges are very real and undeniably frustrating, but they're also entirely manageable. It just takes me a little longer and a bit more effort to get the work done. Despite these hurdles, I've been writing instructional books, publishing articles in music trade magazines, and contributing to blogs and websites for years. So, my dyslexia excuse? It doesn't hold water. If I can do it, so can you.

Tapping Into All 4 Aspects of D.R.U.M. To Overcome Dyslexia And Become A Writer

Living with dyslexia has been a challenging and, at times, a truly crippling experience. As a person who has navigated the tumultuous waters of this learning difference, I can attest to the immense hurdles it presents. Yet, through unwavering determination, self-belief, a positive attitude, patience, and sheer hard work, I have triumphed over these obstacles to achieve the seemingly impossible dream of becoming a published writer.

Dyslexia, a neurodevelopmental disorder that affects reading, writing, and spelling, can cast a long shadow over one's academic and professional pursuits. From a young age, I struggled to grasp the intricacies of written language. Words seemed to dance on the page, making it a formidable challenge to decode and comprehend text. This struggle not only affected my academic performance but also took a toll on my self-esteem.

The journey to becoming a writer was paved with countless moments of frustration and self-doubt. A simple Facebook post can be frustrating and agonizing. However, I refused to let dyslexia define the narrative of my life. Instead, I embraced the idea that success is not determined by the absence of challenges but by the ability to overcome them.

Certainly, numerous successful and famous individuals have not only battled dyslexia but have also triumphed over it. Here are some notable examples:

1. Tom Cruise:
The iconic actor has openly discussed his struggles with dyslexia. Despite this challenge, he has become one of the most successful and recognized actors in Hollywood.

2. Steven Spielberg:
Renowned filmmaker Steven Spielberg faced dyslexia throughout his childhood. Despite his difficulties with reading and writing, he went on to become one of the most celebrated directors in the history of cinema.

3. Richard Branson:
The founder of the Virgin Group, Sir Richard Branson, has dyslexia. He struggled academically but found success in the business world. His dyslexia did not prevent him from becoming a highly successful entrepreneur and philanthropist.

4. Whoopi Goldberg:
The acclaimed actress, comedian, and television host Whoopi Goldberg has dyslexia. She has spoken openly about her experiences and has become an

advocate for dyslexia awareness.

5. Cher:
The iconic singer and actress Cher struggled with dyslexia throughout her school years. Despite these challenges, she has had a remarkable career and is considered a pop culture icon.

6. Sir James Dyson:
The inventor and entrepreneur behind Dyson vacuum cleaners, Sir James Dyson, faced dyslexia in his early years. His innovative spirit and determination led him to revolutionize the home appliance industry.

7. Agatha Christie:
The best-selling mystery novelist Agatha Christie had dyslexia. Her works, including iconic detective stories like "Murder on the Orient Express," continue to captivate readers around the world.

8. Jamie Oliver:
Celebrity chef and restaurateur Jamie Oliver has dyslexia. Despite struggling with reading and writing, he has achieved tremendous success in the culinary world and has become an advocate for healthy eating.

These examples demonstrate that dyslexia does not limit one's potential for success. Instead, it highlights the strength and resilience of individuals who have faced and overcome this challenge to make significant contributions in various fields. Their stories serve as inspiration for others dealing with dyslexia, showing that success is achievable through determination and hard work.

One of the key factors in my journey was an unwavering belief in myself. Despite the setbacks and the occasional feelings of inadequacy, I held onto the conviction that I had something valuable to share with the world. This belief became the driving force that pushed me forward even when the road ahead seemed insurmountable.

Maintaining a positive attitude was equally crucial. It became apparent that dwelling on the difficulties posed by dyslexia would only hinder my progress. Instead, I chose to focus on my strengths and celebrate small victories along the way. This shift in perspective not only boosted my morale but also fueled my determination to keep going.

My first small success came in the form of a music industry magazine called Music Scene International. As I've mentioned in past blogs, my first passion in life is that of being a professional drummer and music educator. As such, I always wanted to contribute to music industry magazines. The pride I felt after seeing my first published article amazing! It was the spark I needed to ignite the flame that would carry me on to become a regularly published columnist for Classic Drummer Magazine.

Learning to read and write with dyslexia is a gradual process that requires time and persistence. I learned to appreciate the incremental improvements, no matter how small, and to trust the journey even when progress seemed slow.

Sheer determination was the cornerstone of my success. Overcoming dyslexia demanded a relentless commitment to hard work and continuous learning. I sought out alternative learning methods, utilized assistive technologies, and developed personalized strategies to navigate the challenges posed by dyslexia.

Becoming a published writer was not just a personal triumph but a testament to the possibility of conquering seemingly insurmountable obstacles. I share my story not as an exception but as an inspiration for others facing their own challenges. Regardless of the nature of your hurdles, whether it's dyslexia or any other obstacle, know that with hard work, self-belief, a positive attitude, patience, and sheer determination, you too can overcome and achieve your dreams.

My journey from the grip of dyslexia to the accomplishment of becoming a published writer has taught me that challenges are not roadblocks but stepping stones to success. Embracing one's unique journey, with all its trials and tribulations, can lead to unexpected triumphs and the realization that the human spirit is indeed resilient and capable of achieving greatness.

Becoming an author and columnist while battling Dyslexia was one of the greatest challenges I've faced, and it required me to lean heavily on all four pillars outlined in this book. Determination was crucial; even writing was agonizing and often embarrassing, so the idea of tackling an entire book or column felt monumental. Still, I pressed on, driven by the desire to share my story and knowledge. Relationships played an essential role, I leaned on trusted friends and colleagues for help with editing, proofreading, graphic design, and other tasks that I couldn't tackle alone. Understanding was vital as I learned to accept that progress would be slow, setbacks were inevitable, and my journey as a writer would take longer than most. Finally, Mentorship was indispensable. My wife guided me in crafting clear, impactful writing, and I reached out to past mentors, like my drum teachers, to refine my ideas and even contribute quotes and forewords to my work. By relying on these four pillars, I turned what seemed like an impossible dream into reality.

Building a Mentorship Culture

For mentorship to truly thrive, it needs to become a cultural norm. As you grow in your career, pay it forward. Offer guidance to those coming up behind you, just as others have done for you. Encourage open dialogue, celebrate achievements, and foster an environment of continuous learning.

Building a mentorship culture requires a collective commitment to growth, collaboration, and mutual support. At its core, mentorship is about fostering relationships where knowledge and experience are shared freely, creating an environment where everyone, mentor and mentee alike, can thrive. It starts with a mindset that values learning over competition and understands that everyone, no matter their level of expertise, has something to contribute. When we encourage a culture of mentorship, we empower individuals to ask questions, seek guidance, and embrace challenges with the confidence that they have the support of a community invested in their success. This culture also nurtures accountability, as mentors lead by example, inspiring others to pay it forward and build a cycle of continuous learning and development.

Ultimately, a mentorship culture strengthens organizations, teams, and personal relationships by fostering trust, collaboration, and shared purpose. It's not just about the immediate benefits of skill-building or problem-solving; it's about creating a legacy of support and empowerment that extends far beyond individual interactions. When we embrace mentorship as a core value, we open the door to innovation, resilience, and a sense of belonging that can transform lives and careers. By investing in others, we not only contribute to their success but also enhance our own, proving that the impact of mentorship is far-reaching and truly invaluable.

In the DRUM framework, mentorship is more than a stepping stone; it's a cornerstone. It's about building a network of support and shared knowledge that benefits not just individuals but the industry as a whole. Whether you're seeking guidance or offering it, remember that mentorship is a journey of shared growth and mutual respect, one note, one beat, one chord at a time.

Chapter 5
The Walk Toward Fear, Start Your Drumming Business Journey

Starting your own drumming business can be as exhilarating as stepping onto the stage for the first time. But for many, fear becomes the invisible wall that holds them back. Whether it's the fear of failure, rejection, or uncertainty, these mental roadblocks can stop you before you even begin. In this chapter, we're going to break through that wall and walk toward fear, because on the other side lies your success.

Embracing the Fear

Every successful musician and business owner has faced fear. It's a natural response to stepping outside your comfort zone. But rather than letting it paralyze you, you must learn to use fear as fuel. If you're nervous about teaching your first drum lesson, recording your first video, or launching your website, that's a good sign, it means you're about to grow.

Take a moment and ask yourself: What exactly am I afraid of? Is it failure? Criticism? Not making enough money? Write these fears down, then challenge them. What's the worst that could happen? More importantly, what's the best that could happen? When you focus on the possibilities instead of the pitfalls, you shift your mindset from fear to action.

Accept That Fear Will Always Be There

The truth is, fear never fully goes away. Even the most seasoned professionals experience self-doubt. Instead of waiting for fear to disappear before taking action, acknowledge its presence and move forward anyway. Fear is simply a signal that you care about what you're doing. If you reframe it as excitement rather than anxiety, you'll find it much easier to take the leap.

Break It Down Into Small Steps

One of the biggest reasons fear holds people back is that they look at the entire journey and feel overwhelmed. Instead of trying to tackle everything at once, break your goals into smaller, manageable steps. If starting a drumming

business feels daunting, begin by teaching just one student, creating one video, or reaching out to one potential client. Each small success builds confidence, making the next step easier.

Surround Yourself With Supportive People

Fear thrives in isolation. If you're trying to do everything alone, it's easy to spiral into self-doubt. Surround yourself with people who believe in you, mentors, fellow drummers, business coaches, or supportive friends. They can offer guidance, encouragement, and even constructive criticism to help you improve. Learning from those who have already walked the path can give you the confidence to keep moving forward.

Trust the Process and Keep Going

Every entrepreneur, including those in the music industry, faces setbacks. You might not get as many students as you hoped right away, your first videos might not go viral, and gigs might not come flooding in immediately. That's okay. Success isn't about never failing; it's about persevering despite the fear of failure. The more you push through discomfort, the more resilient and confident you'll become.

Turn Fear Into Your Greatest Teacher

Fear can either stop you in your tracks or propel you forward, it's your choice. Every challenge you face is an opportunity to learn and grow. When you push past fear, you don't just become a better businessperson; you become a stronger, more resilient musician. Embrace the fear, take action despite it, and watch your drumming business flourish.

Defining Your Drumming Business

Once you've made the decision to start, the next step is defining your business. There are multiple avenues to consider in the drumming industry:

- **Teaching:** *Private lessons, online courses, drum clinics*
- **Session Work:** *Live performances, recording studio gigs, remote drumming*
- **Product Development:** *Books, lesson packs, drum sample libraries*
- **Content Creation:** *YouTube channels, social media drumming content, podcasts*
- **Merchandise & Branding:** *Selling drum-related gear, apparel, and accessories*

You may focus on one of these or blend multiple income streams together. The key is to identify what excites you the most and where your strengths lie. Remember, your drumming business should be an extension of your passion.

Finding Your Unique Selling Point

With so many drummers out there, it's important to carve out your own niche. What makes your approach unique? Do you specialize in a particular style, such as jazz, rock, or metal? Are you an expert at rudiments, groove concepts, or showmanship? Maybe you have a charismatic teaching style or a knack for breaking down complex drumming techniques into simple, digestible lessons. Defining your unique selling point (USP) will help set you apart and attract the right audience to your business.

Building Your Brand Identity

Your brand is more than just a logo, it's the way people perceive you and your work. Think about how you want to be seen in the drumming community. Your website, social media presence, video content, and even the way you communicate with students or clients should all reflect a cohesive and professional image. Choose a name, color scheme, and visual style that represent your personality and message. A strong, recognizable brand will help you gain credibility and make a lasting impression.

Understanding Your Target Audience

Who do you want to serve? If you're teaching, are you focusing on beginners, intermediate players, or advanced drummers looking for a specific skill set? If you're creating online content, are you targeting drummers looking for inspiration, technique breakdowns, or industry insights? The clearer you are about your audience, the better you can tailor your content, lessons, and services to meet their needs. Conduct research, engage with drummers online, and ask for feedback to refine your offerings.

Creating Multiple Revenue Streams

Relying on one income stream can be risky, so consider diversifying. Many successful drummers combine teaching with session work, content creation, or product sales. For example, if you're an educator, you can offer one-on-one lessons while also selling lesson packs or an online course. If you're a session drummer, you can supplement your income by creating drum sample libraries. Having multiple sources of income not only increases your financial stability but also allows you to explore different aspects of your drumming passion.

Staying Adaptable and Open to Growth

The music industry is always evolving, and so should your business. Technology, trends, and audience preferences shift over time, so staying adaptable is key. Keep an eye on industry trends, experiment with new ideas, and continue learning. Whether it's improving your teaching methods, upgrading your recording setup, or expanding your online presence, staying open to growth ensures that your drumming business remains relevant and successful.

Taking Action and Moving Forward

Defining your drumming business is just the beginning. Once you've outlined your vision, it's time to take action. Start small, launch your website, post your first video, or reach out to potential students or clients. Progress happens step by step, and the more you put yourself out there, the more opportunities will come your way. Stay consistent, be patient, and keep refining your approach as you grow. The most successful drummers aren't just talented musicians, they're also determined entrepreneurs who turn their passion into a thriving business.

Taking Action: Start Before You're Ready

One of the biggest myths in business is that you have to have everything figured out before you start. That's simply not true. Many of the most successful drumming entrepreneurs started with what they had and learned along the way.

- **Launch Your First Product or Service:** *Don't wait until everything is perfect. Offer lessons, create a social media page, or book a gig. The experience will teach you more than endless planning.*

- **Start Small, Scale Up:** *If you want to teach, begin with one student. If you want to record drum tracks, start with a simple setup.*

- **Learn as You Go:** *Business, like drumming, is about progress. You'll refine your process over time, but you can't refine what doesn't exist.*

Perfection is the Enemy of Progress

Many drummers hold themselves back because they feel they aren't "ready" to launch. Maybe you think you need a top-tier studio before you can record drum tracks or a professionally designed website before offering lessons. The truth is, waiting for perfection is just another form of procrastination. The best way to improve is through action—start with what you have, and upgrade as you grow.

Overcoming Self-Doubt

Fear of failure or imposter syndrome can stop you from even trying. Thoughts like "What if no one signs up for my lessons?" or "What if my videos don't get views?" can be crippling. Instead of focusing on the worst-case scenario, reframe your mindset. What if someone does sign up? What if your videos inspire just one drummer to improve? Success is built on small wins, and each step forward builds confidence.

Commit to Consistency

Taking action once isn't enough, you need to be consistent. Whether it's posting weekly drumming content, practicing business outreach, or continuously refining your skills, consistency creates momentum. Set a schedule for yourself, even if it's just dedicating a few hours per week to building your business. Over time, these small, consistent efforts will lead to significant growth.

Seek Feedback and Improve

You don't have to do everything perfectly right away, but you do need to learn from your experiences. Ask for feedback from students, clients, or your audience. What do they like? What could be better? Constructive criticism is a tool for improvement, not a reason to quit. The more you adapt and refine, the better your drumming business will become.

Surround Yourself with the Right People

Being around other musicians and entrepreneurs who share your drive can make all the difference. Connect with fellow drummers, business mentors, or online communities. Having a support system will keep you motivated, provide valuable insights, and remind you that you're not alone in the journey. This is exactly what I do, and I have found to be true with The Drummers Education Connection.

Celebrate Every Win

Starting a business is challenging, and it's easy to focus on what's not working. Instead, celebrate every milestone: your first student, your first video, your first sale. Recognizing your progress keeps you motivated and reinforces the idea that you're on the right path. Every step forward is proof that you're turning your drumming passion into a business.

Overcoming Obstacles

Every business journey comes with challenges, but how you handle them determines your success.

- **Dealing with Self-Doubt:** *Imposter syndrome is real. Acknowledge it, but don't let it control you. Remind yourself of your skills, experience, and passion.*

- **Handling Rejection:** *Not everyone will book a lesson with you or buy your product. That's okay. Learn from feedback and move forward.*

- **Managing Finances:** *Start small and reinvest earnings into your business. Keep track of expenses and profits to ensure sustainability.*

Staying Motivated When Progress is Slow

Building a drumming business takes time, and there will be moments when growth feels stagnant. It's easy to get discouraged when your videos don't gain traction, your lesson bookings are low, or your product sales aren't where you'd like them to be. The key is persistence. Success doesn't happen overnight, but every small step brings you closer. Set realistic goals, track your progress, and celebrate your wins, no matter how small.

Balancing Your Time Effectively

Juggling multiple responsibilities, whether it's teaching, gigging, recording, or content creation, can be overwhelming. Prioritization is crucial. Set a schedule that allows you to focus on the most important aspects of your business while maintaining a healthy work-life balance. Time management tools, such as planners or digital calendars, can help you stay organized and avoid burnout.

Adapting to Industry Changes

The music industry is constantly evolving, and so should your business. Whether it's new social media algorithms, changes in online learning trends, or advancements in recording technology, staying informed is key. Keep learning, experimenting, and adapting. The more flexible you are, the better you can position yourself for long-term success.

Handling Competition with Confidence

There will always be other drummers offering lessons, recording tracks, or selling drum-related products. Instead of viewing them as competition, see them as part of the larger drumming community. Focus on what makes you unique. Collaboration, networking, and supporting other musicians can often lead to new opportunities rather than setbacks.

Turning Challenges into Learning Opportunities

Every obstacle is a chance to learn and grow. If a marketing strategy doesn't work, tweak it. If a lesson plan isn't engaging students, refine it. Mistakes and setbacks are inevitable, but they're also valuable. The most successful drummers in business aren't those who never face challenges, it's those who learn from them and keep going.

Never Losing Sight of Your Passion

At the core of your business is your love for drumming. When challenges arise, remind yourself why you started. Passion is what fuels persistence, creativity, and innovation. Stay connected to the joy of playing and sharing your knowledge, and let that drive you through any obstacles that come your way.

The First Step Is Yours to Take

Fear will always be present when stepping into something new, but walking toward it is how you unlock your full potential. Your drumming business won't build itself, it starts with you taking that first step. So whether it's launching a website, promoting your first lesson, or posting your first drum cover, do it today. Start before you're ready, because that's how all great journeys begin.

Embrace the Unknown

Every successful drummer, entrepreneur, or artist once stood where you are now, facing uncertainty, wondering if they were making the right move. The difference between those who succeed and those who don't isn't talent alone; it's the willingness to embrace the unknown and keep pushing forward. Growth happens when you step outside your comfort zone.

Stay Focused on Progress, Not Perfection

It's easy to get caught up in wanting everything to be flawless before you start. But perfection is an illusion, what matters most is progress. Each lesson you teach, each track you record, and each video you upload will make you better. Your business will evolve with experience, and every mistake is just a stepping stone to success.

Build Momentum with Small Wins

Taking action doesn't mean making a giant leap overnight. It means consistently taking small, meaningful steps. Booking your first student, getting your first online follower, or selling your first product might seem minor, but these wins build confidence. Momentum comes from consistent effort, and before you know it, those small wins will add up to something bigger than you imagined.

Find Your Support System

No one succeeds alone. Surround yourself with people who encourage you, whether it's fellow musicians, mentors, or an online community of drummers. Having support during the tough times will keep you going, and connecting with like-minded individuals can open doors to collaborations, opportunities, and new ideas.

Keep Learning and Adapting

The music business is always evolving, and staying open to learning will keep you ahead. Whether it's improving your teaching techniques, mastering new recording software, or understanding social media marketing, continuous growth is key. Be willing to adapt, and see every challenge as a lesson that makes you stronger.

Action Steps:

- **Write down your fears.** *Identify what's holding you back and challenge those thoughts.*

- **Define your drumming business.** *Pick a focus and outline a simple plan.*

- **Take one action today.** *Whether it's creating a social media page, booking a lesson, or recording a video, start now.*

Bart and Rich Redmond at PASIC 2024.

Step Into Your Future with Confidence

Success isn't reserved for a select few, it's available to anyone willing to put in the effort and take that first step. Your drumming business is waiting for you to bring it to life. Don't let fear be the reason you stay stuck. Take action today, no matter how small. Walk toward fear, embrace the journey, and claim the success that's already within you. The world needs your talent, go share it.

Chapter 6
The Rhythm of Success: Integrating DRUM Principles

When you think about drums, you envision a steady rhythm that binds a song together, creating structure and flow. Similarly, success in business requires a rhythm, a synergy of values and actions that bring harmony to your goals and efforts. In this chapter, we will explore how to integrate DRUM principles; Determination, Relationships, Understanding, and Mentorship, to create a sustainable and impactful business. These principles, much like the components of a drum set, each play a vital role in crafting the soundtrack of your success.

Determination: The Driving Beat

Determination is the kickdrum of your business, it's the pulse that keeps everything moving forward. Success requires persistence, even when faced with challenges. Determination isn't just about working hard; it's about working smart, staying focused, and adapting to change.

Real-Life Story: Fred Fischer, a professional drummer and educator from Basie Idaho, faced a major setback when an accident sidelined him with a broken leg. His determination kept him moving forward. Fred shifted his focus solely to online drum lessons, dedicating himself to virtual coaching during his recovery. When he was ready to see students in person again, he successfully resumed in-person teaching. Although he had to step away from live performances and touring for a short time, Fred maintained his extremely positive attitude through a very dark period. By leveraging his existing skills and embracing technology, he kept his income stream steady and continued to inspire his students. His story is a testament to how determination helps overcome obstacles and sustain momentum.

Relationships: The Hi-Hat of Collaboration

The hi-hat's steady rhythm adds nuance and texture to a song, much like relationships add depth to your business. Building strong relationships with clients, collaborators, and your community fosters trust and opens doors to new opportunities. Networking isn't just about exchanging business cards; it's about creating genuine connections that resonate over time.

Real-Life Story: My wife Leah works with a nonprofit animal rescue. Finding financial support can often be a challenge for rescues. She leaned on the relationships she had nurtured with other rescues and local businesses. She helped the rescue secure resources and raise funds by selling Beanie Babies that she had collected over the years at rescue events. These efforts, combined with donations from the community, amplified the rescue's impact. Leah's example shows that meaningful relationships are the backbone of sustainable growth.

Understanding: The Snare of Communication

The snare drum provides clarity and focus in a rhythm, much like understanding provides clarity in business. In most popular music, the snare drum plays on beats 2 and 4, commonly known as the backbeat. This backbeat provides punch and strength to the music, anchoring the groove and driving the song forward. Similarly, understanding your audience, market trends, and your own goals ensures you're hitting the right notes. This principle also includes empathy, and understanding the needs and challenges of your clients and team members.

Real-Life Story: As an educator, I've learned the importance of understanding my students' unique learning styles. When one student struggled with traditional methods, I tailored my approach, integrating visual aids and simplified rhythms. The result? A newfound confidence and passion for drumming in that student. Similarly, understanding and adapting to your audience's needs is a key to business success.

Mentorship: The Ride Cymbal of Guidance

The ride cymbal adds balance and continuity to a song, much like mentorship provides guidance and perspective in business. A good mentor helps you navigate challenges, refine your skills, and unlock your potential. At the same time, mentoring others can solidify your own knowledge and expand your influence.

Real-Life Story: Do Famularo, was not only an amazing drum teacher and taught me technical drumming skills but also imparted lessons on professionalism and perseverance. As stated earlier in this book, Dom was considered "Drumming's Global Ambassador." His mentorship not only shaped and inspired my career, it also shaped and inspired thousands of drummers' careers around the world. He inspired us to give back by mentoring aspiring drummers. Mentorship creates a ripple effect, fostering a community of growth and shared success.

Creating a Sustainable and Impactful Business

The DRUM principles work in concert to create a sustainable business model. Determination keeps you moving, relationships open doors, understanding ensures you're meeting needs, and mentorship builds a legacy. Together, they create a rhythm that's both impactful and enduring.

Practical Tips for Applying DRUM Principles:

1. **Set SMART Goals:** *Align your determination with Specific, Measurable, Achievable, Relevant, and Time-bound objectives.*

Setting SMART goals is essential for channeling your determination into focused and productive efforts. Specific goals ensure clarity, leaving no room for ambiguity about what you want to achieve. Measurable objectives allow you to track your progress and celebrate milestones along the way, keeping motivation high. Goals should be Achievable, challenging enough to push your limits but realistic enough to avoid frustration. Relevance ensures your goals align with your broader vision and values, ensuring that your efforts contribute meaningfully to your long-term aspirations. Finally, Time-bound goals create a sense of urgency, encouraging consistent action and preventing procrastination. Together, these components provide a roadmap for success, transforming vague ambitions into actionable steps and turning determination into tangible results.

2. **Network Authentically:** *Focus on building genuine relationships rather than transactional ones.*

Networking authentically is about creating meaningful connections that extend beyond mere transactions or self-interest. Genuine relationships are built on trust, mutual respect, and shared values, which foster a sense of collaboration and community. Instead of approaching networking with a "What can I get?" mindset, focus on understanding others' needs, goals, and challenges. Offer value, whether through advice, resources, or support and be genuinely invested in their success. Authentic connections tend to be long-lasting, opening doors to opportunities that might not arise from superficial interactions. These relationships often evolve into partnerships or alliances that benefit everyone involved. By prioritizing authenticity, you create a network that not only supports your professional growth but also enriches your personal journey. In the long run, people remember those who genuinely care, making authentic networking a cornerstone of sustainable success.

3. **Research and Reflect:** *Continuously seek to understand your market, audience, and personal growth areas.*

In the music business, the landscape is ever-changing, making it essential to prioritize research and reflection. Staying attuned to your market means understanding industry trends, such as shifts in streaming platforms, new technologies, or emerging genres, so you can adapt your strategies and remain relevant. Knowing your audience is equally critical; take time to analyze their preferences, listening habits, and values to tailor your work and marketing efforts effectively. Personal growth is another cornerstone–assessing your skills, identifying areas for improvement, and seeking opportunities for learning, whether through workshops, collaborations, or mentorship. Reflection allows you to evaluate your progress, measure the success of your efforts, and refine your approach. By combining diligent research with honest self-assessment, you can navigate the complexities of the music industry with confidence, ensuring your career evolves alongside your audience and the broader market.

4. **Seek and Offer Mentorship:** *Find a mentor who aligns with your goals and values, and look for opportunities to mentor others.*

Mentorship is a powerful tool in the music business, offering a bridge between experience and aspiration. Seeking a mentor who aligns with your goals and values provides guidance tailored to your unique path, whether you're navigating the complexities of recording contracts, refining your stage presence, or expanding your creative repertoire. A mentor can share industry insights, provide constructive feedback, and help you avoid common pitfalls, accelerating your growth and confidence. Equally important is offering mentorship to others. By sharing your knowledge and experiences, you not only give back to the community but also reinforce your own understanding and leadership skills. Mentorship creates a cycle of growth and inspiration, fostering a culture of collaboration in an industry that often feels competitive. Whether you're seeking wisdom from those ahead of you or sharing it with those just starting out, mentorship is a cornerstone of long-term success in the music business.

Success, much like music, depends on rhythm and harmony to create something greater than the sum of its parts. In music, rhythm provides structure and flow, while harmony adds depth and emotion. Similarly, a thriving business requires a well-coordinated balance between determination, relationships, understanding, and mentorship. These DRUM principles work together to form a cohesive framework that drives growth and resilience. When approached with intention, these elements not only create a sustainable enterprise but also set a tempo that others want to emulate, turning your business into a source of inspiration and innovation.

Determination is the foundation, the driving beat that keeps your business moving forward even in the face of challenges. It's the energy that propels you through tough times, helping you adapt and innovate. Determination isn't about blind perseverance; it's about staying focused on your goals while remaining flexible enough to navigate unexpected changes. By cultivating a strong sense of purpose and persistence, you set the rhythm for success, ensuring that your business doesn't lose momentum, even when the path gets tough.

Relationships add the harmony that makes the rhythm of determination resonate more deeply. Building meaningful connections with clients, partners, and your community creates opportunities for collaboration and mutual support. Strong relationships foster trust, open doors, and add stability to your business. They are the networks that amplify your reach and the bonds that sustain you during challenging times. Just as harmony in music brings different notes together in a pleasing way, relationships bring together diverse strengths and perspectives, enriching your business and helping it grow.

Understanding and mentorship round out the composition, adding clarity and guidance to your efforts. Understanding ensures that your goals align with the needs of your audience and market. It helps you adapt to changes, refine your approach, and maintain relevance.

Mentorship, on the other hand, provides the wisdom and perspective needed to navigate complex challenges while also giving you the chance to uplift others. Together, these principles create a holistic strategy for success. The DRUM framework is not just an abstract philosophy, it's a practical, actionable approach that, when embraced fully, transforms your business into a finely tuned masterpiece. Finally, the DRUM principles aren't just theoretical concepts; they are actionable steps that, when practiced, lead to success stories of their own.

Chapter 7
Conclusion - Reflections on Your Journey

As we come to the end of this journey through Drum Up Your Business, it's important to take a moment to reflect on everything you've learned and the steps you've taken toward growing your musical career and business. Whether you're a seasoned professional or just starting out, this book has served as a roadmap to navigate the complexities of building a thriving music business. From developing your craft to marketing your brand, each chapter provides insights that can help propel your career forward.

The journey you're on is uniquely yours. It's shaped by your experiences, your passion, and the decisions you make. As we've explored the critical elements of success, from networking to setting up a strong business foundation, from identifying your target audience to managing your finances, what remains clear is this: the power to grow your business lies in your hands. The music industry is constantly evolving, but the fundamentals of building strong relationships, providing value, and staying true to your artistic vision never change.

In reflecting on your journey, remember that growth is not always linear. There will be highs and lows, moments of uncertainty, and breakthroughs. The key is consistency, continuing to take steps forward, no matter how small. Each gig, each conversation, and each social media post contributes to the foundation of your business. Stay focused on your goals and keep learning from both successes and failures.

Taking Action to Drum Up Your Business

The most crucial takeaway from this book is that taking action is the driving force behind any business success. You've now armed yourself with knowledge and strategies to implement– but the next step is to put everything into practice.

- **Set Clear Goals:** *Don't just dream about success; set concrete, measurable goals. Whether it's landing a certain number of gigs per month or growing your social media following, having a clear target will give you direction and purpose.*

- **Build Your Network:** *Your relationships are one of your greatest assets. Invest time in meeting new people, collaborating with other musicians, and connecting with industry professionals who can help open doors.*

- **Stay Consistent:** *Consistency in your marketing efforts, content creation, and performances will help establish your brand and reputation. Your audience should know what to expect from you, and you should deliver on that promise with every interaction.*

- **Continue Learning:** *The music business is ever-evolving, so keep learning. Attend workshops, read books, take courses, and always stay curious. The more you learn, the better equipped you'll be to navigate challenges and seize new opportunities.*

Taking action means embracing both the excitement and the responsibility that comes with managing your business. By applying the principles shared in this book, you will start to see tangible results. Progress may not always be immediate, but with persistence and dedication, you'll find yourself building the business you've always envisioned.

It's the Final Curtain

As I sit down to write the final words of this book, I'm struck by how deeply personal this journey has been. "Drum Up Your Business" wasn't just an idea for a book; it was a way for me to channel the lessons of a lifetime spent in the music business. This industry has given me so much, a career filled with incredible highs, challenging lows, and countless moments in between. It's a journey I wouldn't trade for anything, and my hope is that this book serves as a guide for you to navigate your own path with purpose and passion.

When I began writing, my primary motivation was to help others avoid some of the pitfalls that tripped me up along the way. The music business can be a minefield, filled with uncertainty, tough decisions, and moments of self-doubt. But it's also a place where determination, creativity, and authenticity can lead to a fulfilling and impactful career. My goal was to share not just the strategies that have worked for me, but also the mindset shifts that I've found to be essential for success.

The Sam Morrison Band playing to another capacity crowd in Michigan.

Determination

One of the most valuable lessons I've learned is the power of determination. Whether it's perfecting your craft, landing that dream gig, or building a sustainable business, determination is what separates those who thrive from those who falter. It's about showing up, even when it's hard, even when it feels like no one is watching. Keep setting goals, stay focused, and push through the moments of doubt. Determination isn't just about getting where you want to go; it's about proving to yourself that you're capable of more than you imagined.

Building Relationships

If there's one truth that resonates across every chapter of this book, it's this: relationships are everything. Whether it's your bandmates, collaborators, mentors, or the fans who support your art, the connections you build will define your career. Invest time and energy into cultivating genuine relationships. Listen, communicate, and show up for others. The people you meet along the way will become your allies, your teachers, and your biggest advocates. Remember, the music business is as much about people as it is about music.

Learning and Growth

The moment you think you've mastered it all is the moment you've stopped growing. Success in any business, especially music, requires a commitment to lifelong learning. Whether it's expanding your knowledge of the industry, honing your technical skills, or gaining deeper self-awareness, the pursuit of growth is what keeps you moving forward. Don't be afraid to step out of your comfort zone. Try new things. Make mistakes. Every experience, good or bad, is an opportunity to learn more about yourself and your craft.

Understanding and Mentorship

Understanding is the glue that holds everything together. It's about recognizing the bigger picture, how your music fits into the world, how the business operates, and how your actions affect others. And with understanding comes the responsibility to mentor and support the next generation. Just as others have guided you, you have the power to be a guiding light for someone else. Share your knowledge, offer encouragement, and be the kind of mentor you wish you had when you were starting out.

Overcoming Addiction

Addiction can feel like a heavy chain, holding you down and keeping you from living your best life. If you're reading this and feel that you need help, let this be your sign: you don't have to face this alone. Admitting you need help is a powerful first step toward healing. No matter where you are in life, reaching out for support can open doors to a brighter future. Whether it's confiding in a trusted friend, contacting a counselor, or joining a recovery group, help is everywhere, and you are not alone in this fight.

The music business, like many other industries, is not only filled with stories of addiction but also with incredible tales of recovery. Countless artists and professionals have faced their demons, sought help, and come out stronger on the other side. Their journeys are testaments to the fact that recovery is possible. These individuals now serve as inspirations, proving that life after addiction can be not only manageable but fulfilling. If you're struggling, remember that the people you admire in the industry might have walked a similar path and found the courage to seek change.

There is absolutely no shame in seeking help. In fact, it's a sign of strength. Addiction thrives in silence and isolation, but recovery begins when you take steps toward connection and honesty. Many support networks are designed specifically for people in creative fields, understanding the unique challenges you might face. Whether it's Alcoholics Anonymous, Narcotics Anonymous, or programs tailored to your needs, resources exist to guide you. As the saying goes, "Seek and you will find."

Remember, addiction does not define you. You are not your mistakes, and your past does not determine your future. With the right support, you can reclaim your life, rediscover your passion, and find a new purpose. It won't always be easy, but the rewards of sobriety, peace, health, and the ability to truly connect with others are immeasurable. Take that first step today; there is a world of people and resources ready to help you. You're worth it.

Becoming a Better You

Ultimately, all of these elements, determination, relationships, learning, understanding, and mentorship, are about one thing: becoming the best version of yourself. The music business, like life, is a mirror. It reflects back the effort, passion, and authenticity you bring to it. By focusing on these principles, you'll not only build a thriving career but also grow as a person. And that, in the end, is the real goal.

Thank you for joining me on this journey. Whether you're a seasoned professional or just starting out, I hope this book has given you the tools and inspiration to navigate your path with confidence and clarity. Remember, success isn't about avoiding every stumble–it's about getting back up, learning, and continuing forward. You have everything you need within you to make your dreams a reality.

Final Words of Encouragement

As you embark on this exciting chapter of your career, I want to leave you with some final words of encouragement.

First, believe in your vision. The path to success is rarely easy, but when you're committed to what you do, that passion will resonate with your audience and collaborators. Even when you face obstacles, stay grounded in your purpose and keep moving forward.

Second, embrace failure as a lesson. Mistakes are a natural part of growth, and each setback offers a valuable lesson. Use these experiences to sharpen your skills, refine your strategies, and become better at what you do.

Lastly, remember that success doesn't happen overnight. It's a journey that takes time, effort, and resilience. But the rewards, personal fulfillment, financial stability, and a lasting impact on your audience will make it all worthwhile. Also, take note that a lot of time, success doesn't look like you thought it would. Be mindful and enjoy where you're at. This is a journey, not a destination, and the horizon is always moving forward. Keep drumming up your business with confidence and perseverance, and you'll create something lasting and meaningful.

Your future in the music business is bright, and this is just the beginning. Keep pushing boundaries, stay focused on your goals, and remember that every step you take is a step closer to achieving your dreams.

Keep drumming, keep hustling, and most importantly, keep believing in yourself. The world is waiting for your music.

With gratitude and belief in your journey,

Chapter 8
Resources and Tools

As you work to build and grow your music business, the right resources and tools can make all the difference. Below, I've compiled a list of valuable tools, worksheets, and additional learning resources that will help you achieve your goals. Whether you're looking to improve your goal-setting process, expand your network, or deepen your industry knowledge, these resources will support you along the way.

Worksheets for Goal Setting, Networking, and Strategy

These worksheets will help you apply the concepts discussed in *Drum Up Your Business* and turn them into actionable steps. They are designed to help you track progress, set measurable goals, and stay focused on your long-term vision.

1. **Goal Setting Worksheet**
This worksheet is designed to help you clarify your goals, break them down into smaller, actionable steps, and track your progress over time. It includes sections for long-term and short-term goals, as well as specific action items that will help you achieve them. By filling this out, you'll gain clarity on where you want your music business to go and how to get there.

Key Sections:
- *Long-Term Goals*
- *Short-Term Goals*
- *Monthly Action Steps*
- *Weekly Tasks and Progress Tracking*

2. **Networking Strategy Worksheet**
Building relationships is one of the most crucial aspects of any music business. This worksheet will help you strategize and organize your networking efforts. It includes sections to define who you want to connect with, how to approach them, and follow-up strategies to ensure lasting relationships.

Key Sections:

- *Key Industry Contacts*
- *Networking Approach (Events, Online, etc.)*
- *Follow-Up Plans*
- *Collaboration Opportunities*

3. **Business Strategy Worksheet**
   This worksheet will help you outline your business plan, identify your unique value proposition, and create a roadmap for success. It includes sections for market research, pricing strategies, and an analysis of your strengths and weaknesses. This tool will help you ensure that your business is built on a solid foundation.

Key Sections:

- *Market Research and Target Audience*
- *Pricing and Revenue Streams*
- *SWOT Analysis (Strengths, Weaknesses, Opportunities, Threats)*
- *Marketing and Branding Strategy*

Recommended Reading and Learning Resources

To continue expanding your knowledge and staying ahead in the music industry, I've put together a list of recommended books, websites, and online resources that will help you deepen your understanding of the business side of music. These resources cover everything from music marketing to personal growth, and will equip you with the tools you need to succeed.

1. **The Rhythmic Journey: Unleashing the Beat Within**
   by Bart Robley
   This book offers a deep dive into the art of drumming and the creative journey behind making music. Whether you're a beginner or a seasoned professional, The Rhythmic Journey provides valuable lessons on how to unlock your musical potential, refine your skills, and apply your passion to real-world success.

2. **The War of Art** *by Steven Pressfield*
   A game-changer for creative entrepreneurs, The War of Art tackles the internal struggles that hold us back from doing our best work. Pressfield's

focus on resistance– the invisible force that keeps us from realizing our potential– will resonate with any musician who has ever felt blocked or unsure. The lessons in this book are indispensable for anyone who wants to push through procrastination and self-doubt to build a successful career in music.

Online Learning Platforms

- **Berklee Online (https://online.berklee.edu)**
  Berklee College of Music's online programs offer a variety of courses focused on music business, music production, and more. These courses are perfect for musicians looking to deepen their industry knowledge.

- **Coursera (https://www.coursera.org)**
  Coursera offers several courses on entrepreneurship, marketing, and music business that you can take at your own pace.

- **Skillshare (https://www.skillshare.com)**
  Learn practical skills, including social media marketing, business strategy, and more, from experienced instructors.

Podcasts and Online Communities

- **Drummers Education Connection Podcast**
  Tune into the Drummers Education Connection Podcast to hear from top drummers and industry professionals about how to build your career in music. Whether you're looking for advice on technique, business, or inspiration, this podcast provides valuable insights for drummers of all levels. You can access episodes at DrummersEdCon.com.

- **The DIY Musician Podcast**
  A great podcast for independent musicians looking for tips on music marketing, building a fanbase, and monetizing their music.

- **Music Business Worldwide**
  https://www.musicbusinessworldwide.com)

Stay updated with the latest news and trends in the global music industry, including information on record labels, streaming services, and emerging technologies.

Websites for Music Business Tools

- **Songtrust (https://www.songtrust.com)**
  A platform for managing your music publishing rights and ensuring you're collecting royalties for your work.

- **ReverbNation (https://www.reverbnation.com)**
  ReverbNation offers tools for musicians to manage their online presence, promote their music, and book gigs.

- **Bandcamp (https://www.bandcamp.com)**
  An excellent platform for musicians to sell their music directly to fans while keeping a large portion of the profits.

Industry News & Updates

- **Billboard (https://www.billboard.com)**
  The go-to resource for the latest music industry news, chart rankings, and trends.

- **Hypebot (https://www.hypebot.com)**
  Hypebot offers updates, insights, and advice for musicians looking to grow their careers and navigate the digital music landscape.

By leveraging these resources, worksheets, and recommended learning materials, you'll be better equipped to build and sustain a successful music business. The key to success is staying proactive, continuously learning, and applying what you learn to your daily efforts. The tools provided here are designed to help you take the next step, whether that's setting concrete goals, strengthening your network, or expanding your knowledge of the business.

If you're ready to dive deeper into your music career, explore the Drummers Education Connection Podcast for more insights from industry professionals. And don't forget to check out BartRobley.com for additional resources and updates about upcoming projects. Keep drumming, keep learning, and, most importantly, keep pushing your business forward. The music world is waiting for your contribution!

By using the tools provided in this section and exploring the recommended reading and learning resources, you are taking the next step toward building a successful and sustainable career in the music business. Stay consistent, keep learning, and don't forget to take action every day— your future success begins now!

Goal setting worksheet

My name:	Date:

Short Term Goals

Long Term Goals

Monthly Action Steps	Weekly Tasks

What will I do to achieve my goals?	How will I monitor my process?

Tasks that will lead to my goal

Date	Tasks	✓

BartRobley.com

Business Strategy Worksheet

My name:	Date:

Target Audience

Pricing & Revenue Streams

SWOT Analysis (Streghths, Weaknesses, Opportunities, Threats)

Marketing & Branding Strategy

Notes

Network Strategy Worksheet

My name:	Date:

Key Industry Contacts

Key Industry Contacts

Networking Approach (Events Online Etc.)

Follow Up Plans

Colaboration Opportunities

Acknowledgments

I would like to begin by expressing my deepest gratitude to my wife, Leah Robey, for her unwavering love, support, and encouragement throughout life. Her belief in me has been a constant source of strength and inspiration.

A heartfelt thank you to Sam Morrison, Gregg Kasparian, Karl Sanger, Walk Thompson, David Kurtz, Rick Dains, Todd McTavish, Dusty Watson, Chris Brady, and all my dear friends and colleagues who have shared their wisdom, expertise, and camaraderie along the way. Your support has been invaluable in shaping my path.

The members of The Drummers Education Connection, Jeremy Steinkoler, Rick Stojak, Chip Ritter. Your friendships mean the world to me, and your insight is more inspirational than you know.

I am grateful for the friendship and mentorship of Ted Fulet, Ralph Humphrey, Dom Famularo, Bill Hartell, Rob Heskett, Robert Slack, and Gregg Bissonette, whose dedication to the craft has inspired me in countless ways.

The companies who have backed my play and helped me create my sound for years, Aquarian Drumheads, Gretsch Drums, Sabian Cymbals, Vic Firth Sticks, Gibraltar Hardware, and Audix Microphones, your commitment to quality gear, have made all the difference in my playing and teaching. A special thank you to Andrew Shreve, Chris Stankee, Joe Bergamini, Rob Wallis, Rich Redmond, Adam Parson, and Michael Vail Blum for your collaboration and inspiration.

Hudson Music, Centerstream Music, Ron Middlebrook, and Roger Palmateer for their continued support and contribution to the drumming community.

In my previous book, The Rhythmic Journey, I was honored to have the legendary Dom Famularo write the foreword. Dom was a giant in our business, an unparalleled force of positivity and inspiration whose spirit continues to resonate within the drumming community. As I began work on Drum Up Your Business, there was only one person who came to mind to write the foreword: Steve Jacobs. Steve is not only an incredible drummer but also one of the most respected figures in the drumming industry. With years of experience as a sales representative, Steve has become a beacon of positivity, wisdom, and energy, touching the lives of so many. Steve, thank you for your invaluable contribution to this project and for bringing your unique perspective to these pages.

Lastly, I am grateful to all the drummers, musicians, and educators who have influenced me over the years. This book would not have been possible without the collective wisdom and inspiration I have gained from each of you. Thank you for supporting me in my journey, and for inspiring others to do the same.

Bart Robley has presented a realistic and practical approach to what it means to be a professional drummer. His years of hard work, determination, business acumen and diligent practice have earned him many musical opportunities doing what he loves to do... playing drums and making a good living at it! There is no quick way to success and the quote "If it were easy, everyone would be doing it" holds true.. This book clearly outlines what it takes to not only develop one's drumming skills and to keep pushing through the tough times but also how important it is to handle the business side of things in a professional manner. **'Drum Up Your Business'** is a must read for every aspiring drummer!

Wishing you all the best in your musical endeavors.

Steve Distanislao
Studio and Touring Drummer
(David Gilmour, David Crosby, Don Felder Band)

"Every page of **"DRUM Up Your Business"** features a treasure trove of wisdom and gems that will help any drummer develop a deeper and more robust career. By using a crystal clear acronym, Bart concisely explains how determination, relationships, understanding and mentorship can be used to create a lifelong drumming business. Concepts like mindset, resilience, networking, emotional intelligence, and overcoming obstacles are all addressed expertly by someone who has decades of experience in all aspects of the drumming world. In fact, this book would be a useful resource for any musician. Bart has written another amazing book!"

Rich Redmond

Drummer, Speaker, Author, Host, Emcee, Actor
(Jason Aldean/Sessions/Clinics)
www.richredmond.com

More Great Drumming Books by Bart Robley

The Rhythmic Journey

with a foreword by Dom Famularo

Written with passion and expertise by acclaimed veteran drummer, studio musician, and educator Bart Robley, this book takes readers on a captivating journey through the vast world of percussion, highlighting the significance of rhythm in personal growth, creativity, and self-expression.

ISBN: 9781574244175 - 120 PGS

Drummer's Survival Guide

Pre-Prepped Charts for Writing, Teaching, Learning & Reference

With four of the most common ride patterns already written, in both one- and two-bar phrases, this book cuts transcription time in half: all you do is fill in the bass and snare drum patterns.

ISBN: 9781574242522 - Spiral Bound

Rockin' Poppin' Snare Drum, Vol. 1

Rhythm Fundamentals

In this book you will learn to read everything from quarter-note sticking patterns all the way to rebounded sixteenth notes, and then it's on to rudimental drum rolls. The 40 essential drum rudiments are also included in the front of the book.

ISBN: 9781574242706

CENTERSTREAM®

Centerstream-USA.com